Viv Richards

Viv Richards

VIV RICHARDS
WITH
DAVID FOOT

WORLD'S WORK LTD
The Windmill Press
Kingswood Surrey

ACKNOWLEDGEMENTS

The authors and publisher gratefully acknowledge photographs
by Patrick Eagar which appear on pages 109 (foot), 112, 115,
118,121,124,127 and also other photographs kindly lent by Peter
McCombe.

First published in 1979 by
World's Work Ltd
The Windmill Press, Kingswood, Tadworth, Surrey.
Second impression 1979
Filmset and printed in Great Britain by
BAS Printers Limited, Over Wallop, Hampshire.

Hardback edition SBN 437 14470 4
Paperback edition SBN 437 14471 2

Contents

Introduction
BY DAVID FOOT

Isaac Vivian Alexander Richards is the most attractive sort of hero.

He is a fallible genius. He flirts with the record book when, we suspect, he could monopolise it. His cricket, always potent and often pure, is unwaveringly instinctive.

In four years or so he became arguably the best batsman in the world. This is not extravagant journalistic talk. It is the considered opinion of respected pundits, fellow professionals—their judgments too easily influenced at times by cynicism, cautious praise and even envy—spectators and friends who sycophantically follow his fours and foibles.

Vivian Richards's lissom grace has been compared to Worrell and his pugnacious power to Weekes. At the County Ground in Bristol, where memories are long and loving, he has suddenly paraded a succession of poetic cover boundaries, wickedly reminding his rare detractors that he can score just as sweetly through the offside, and generating spontaneous simulations of how Wally Hammond did it the same way.

He is usually in a hurry. 'I occupy the crease to score runs', he says with simple logic, at the same time implying criticism of others whose apparent self-perpetuating philosophy of batsmanship bores and baffles him. He never publicly indicts another cricketer—not even the occasional Australian who has been known to let fly an intimidating oath at him to complement a bouncer.

Vivian plays his cricket like a West Indian. There's a calypso rhythm in his swing. He boyishly enjoys hitting sixes best of all just as he did more than a decade ago when his friends from the

7

grammar school back in Antigua ran joyfully to retrieve the ball. Yet oddly, he plays like a Somerset man, too. It's unthinkable, one feels, that he could have joined any other county. He happily agrees as each April he returns to his Taunton friends and favourite fish-and-chip shop. The people are warm and visibly rural. He likes the cosy market-town pubs and the obsessional cricket banter although he shies away from the Packer politics. 'I owe so much to Somerset. They gave me my real chance', he will say in a moment of confidence. When he says that he is being both loyal and honest; there's nothing remotely devious about him. If he thought Somerset C.C.C. were run by a bunch of amateurs ready to cheat him over a contract, he'd quickly tell you. He doesn't and there is mutual affection—and so there should be.

He rides the idolatry uneasily. His modesty is in no way affected. He stays out of sight in the dressing room after matches because he still can't cope with all the well-intentioned back-slapping. Nor does he like the parasites and hangers-on who crowd the bar afterwards and latch on with fawning bonhomie to current stars of professional sport.

Somerset has not won a title in more than a hundred years. Its history is devoid of trophies but not of great cricketers. The late Harold Gimblett was one and he, like Richards, was characteristically fallible: he was apt to swish with reckless indifference at the away-swinger or look for a four off the last ball before lunch if it was unwisely pitched up to him. Gimblett himself relished Richards in frenetic flight; Richards would have enjoyed Gimblett. With apt and felicitous timing, the applause from Richards's boundaries could be clearly heard during the memorial service for Gimblett at the nearby St James church in Taunton.

Vivian Richards steeled himself to win something for Somerset in 1978. He failed and his self-reproach, manifested in an extraordinarily dramatic and poignant scene in the dressing room, is graphically told by himself later in this book.

Various people can claim some of the credit for bringing him to this country and, in effect, preparing him for an international career of such exhilarating impact.

8

A stray word or two of praise from Colin Cowdrey began the process. 'I'd played against him twice in Antigua', Cowdrey recalls. 'I particularly remember the second time. There was this delightful young fellow with a jaunty air and cheerful approach. He was wearing his cap in a special way that appealed to me. And he had a big smile to go with it.

'The crowd were so obviously behind him. I got the impression that he was already something of a hero although I'd hardly heard of him myself. I noticed the same crowd feeling when Andy Roberts, also from Antigua, was running up to bowl that day. Vivian, I remember, was so natural—strong and quick.'

And Colin Cowdrey's passing lines of admiration, contained in a report carried by 'The Cricketer' sent Len Creed, a Bath bookmaker, hurrying out to Antigua, ostensibly on his holidays.

Len's capture is now part of West Country folklore. It was, whatever the understandably sceptical committeemen may have said at the time, a remarkable piece of opportunism and judgment—and financial courage.

Colin Atkinson, the former Somerset skipper who is now the president, was chairman at the time. He was one of those who hesitated when Len phoned from the West Indies. 'I tell the story against myself', says Atkinson.

There was perhaps, after all, a suggestion that Len Creed's judgment of a cricketer at this level was unproven.

'When Len rang first, seeking the necessary authority to bring his discovery back, I didn't want to involve the county club in unnecessary expense and I was reluctant to use up a special registration on the recommendation of just one man.

'He rang me a second time. Would we, he now wondered, be agreeable for him to bring Vivian over on the understanding that if the newcomer was good enough we'd reimburse him? It seemed a very good and fair deal. I said Yes.'

Colin Atkinson adds with sheepish good humour, 'How were we to know Len would come up with a world beater? He has dined out on it a few times since!'

Millfield's headmaster was quickly won over, of course. 'I can think of no finer example for any young player. If I wanted to show any of my boys how they ought to bat, I'd take them to see Vivian. He has near-perfect technique and immense power. And he gets into position earlier than anyone I've ever seen.' There's a perceptible wince in the expression of David Graveney, Gloucestershire's slow left-arm bowler. It could be said that Graveney, among the most intelligent and amiable of county cricketers, speaks from painful experience. He once conceded five sixes to Richards on a Sunday afternoon. 'He always looks to me as though he has decided what to do before the bowler even starts his run-up. He has incredible time to spare.'

The day he savaged Graveney, Richards was in sight of a record number of John Player League sixes. It looked like a formality for him. So easy, in fact, that he unconcernedly ran down the wicket to Graveney's first ball. He missed it—and so did wicket keeper Andy Stovold.

The slow bowler had first met Richards in the West Indian's early days with Lansdown, the Bath club side paternally watched over by Len Creed. 'I was struck by the way he stood and the way he batted across the front foot. He had all the characteristics of a very strong leg-side player. And that meant, as a slow left arm bowler, I was heading for trouble.'

It also meant that straight balls that theoretically demanded respect were pushed contemptuously away to mid-wicket or mid-on.

David Graveney, like so many county cricketers and Test opponents who vainly tried to bowl to their field, invariably lost the psychological battle with Richards.

'He made 240 against us and told me the night before that he'd be making 200. That wasn't arrogance. I got to the state of seeing him on the morning of a match and asking: "How many sixes today, Viv?" '

What did Brian Close make of him? In fact, he took to him the moment they were introduced—more warmly, I fancy, than he took to one or two of the other pros at Taunton and before that at Headingley.

Close, nurtured in Yorkshire where wickets were never wantonly sacrificed, suddenly found himself handling an easy-going young West Indian, largely uncoached and with not much knowledge of the ritual of championship cricket in England.

'I took Vivian round in my car and we talked cricket all the time. Never once was he difficult to handle. I gave him a bit of stick once or twice because of a lack of concentration. But that shortcoming could be put down to a sort of naiveté on his part about first class cricket and what was expected.

'He was from the start so unbelievably calm, with none of the natural West Indian exuberance, as far as I could see.'

Close remained captain of Somerset until 1977 and he continues to savour the memory of Richards's hooking and the shots he played off his toes.

Richards could, however, look languid, almost indolent, between the wickets. The skipper must at times have heard the collective gasps at Taunton, Bath and Weston as this great batsman squeezed in after a suicidally strolling single.

'Viv could be exceptionally fast when he wanted to', he recalls with twinkling emphasis. 'There was this attitude of mind, I felt, as if he was saying he could hit so many fours that there was really no point in taking singles!'

Opinion on Brian Close as a county captain may vary sharply. Richards's admiration is apparent in this book. It goes back to the days when the intrepid Yorkshireman was squaring up to Hall and Griffiths. Richards missed hardly a ball of that tough confrontation as it was relayed over a crackling radio set.

Vivian gives a touching account of the occasion Close first acknowledged the newcomer's promise. Swansea seems an unlikely venue for a Yorkshireman and an Antiguan to discover an initial rapport which never lessened.

'This bloke', Brian Close tells me with honest deliberation, 'is the most exciting player I have ever run up against—and remember I have seen many of the great players. If Vivian was batting, you didn't want to miss a shot.'

Close clearly knew how to keep a fatherly eye on him. But how coachable was he? A player of this exceptional talent could surely inhibit many a coach.

Peter Robinson, who took over from Tom Cartwright at Somerset as county coach, says frankly: 'You don't tell a player like this when he is doing something wrong—he comes to you. Viv had a little bit of trouble with his batting when he returned in the April of 1978. He'd go into the nets on a Sunday morning and David Gurr and myself would bowl to him. 'We talked about it. He has always been easy to talk to. His pick-up had got a bit wider than it was. Viv soon put that right.'

Like Greg Chappell before him at Somerset, Richards was quick to adapt and work out the different game in England. Privately he admitted how disconcerting it could be at the start of a county cricket season after several months on the hard, reliable strips of the West Indies or Australia.

Australia has always had good leg-side players. But opponents in England are still astonished by Richards's prodigious on-side strength—the way he strikes the ball, often, from middle and off.

One well-known umpire said to Peter Robinson: 'Christ, how does he do it? He's only got to miss it and he'll be LBW.'

He very rarely does miss it, of course. It's noticeable how sides have tried to counter him. In the one-day games they pack the leg-side with six fielders and hopefully wait for him to get himself out.

Yet, as TV pundits as well as perplexed bowlers will agree, he is quite capable of leaning on an exquisite cover drive, as perfectly executed as anything you will see in the contemporary game.

Robinson highlights that magnificently muscular six over extra cover—as demonstrated to gasping and almost disbelieving television viewers during the Gillette Cup semi-final match with Essex in 1978—that Richards can daringly reveal at a time when the bowler is determinedly aiming at leg stump. 'Somehow he makes the room for it. You don't coach that kind of thing. Vivian is a wonderful improviser.'

In his pre-Somerset days, Vivian was once flown to England for a coaching session at Alf Gover's school' 'When I gave him his first net', says Alf, 'it was obvious to me that I had a young player with a touch of class that leads to great batting. He was well balanced, had a superb sense of timing and a pair of good hands to put the power into his shots'.

But it was clear to Gover that this very quiet lad from Antigua lacked experience against the outswinger and off-spinner. 'I worked on him and he showed a quick understanding of the methods to be used in attacking both types of bowling. We also concentrated on "using the field"—hitting on both sides of the wicket as well as straight.

'He was, I remember, a modest chap and a pleasure to coach.'

These summer evenings at Taunton, after a day's cricket, Vivian occasionally wanders round to the Westgate Inn, kept now by Roy Marshall, the former Hampshire opening batsman who was born in Barbados. Roy, who also coaches at King's, Taunton, was as a batsman forceful and stylish. His cricketing discussions with Richards, at times long after the customers have gone home, are invariably intense. He confesses himself amazed, for instance, at the way medium-paced bowlers have to put a mid-wicket back on the boundary in an attempt to curb Richards.

Flawless timing . . . strong hands . . . powerful shoulders . . . comfortable stance . . . Marshall says the Antiguan has all of this. 'I have never seen anyone hit the ball so hard and with so little effort. Plenty of players can hit hard but not with Vivian's apparent lack of effort.'

Vivian Richards has ended games with a theatrical flourish, stage-managing his six into the car park. He has put the ball between the tombstones in St James churchyard at Taunton and into the gents' lavatories although not, curiously enough, into the River Tone, the one-time speciality of Arthur Wellard.

Just occasionally he has played an exclusively defensive role. Peter Robinson cites a match against Middlesex when Richards unselfishly kept one end going while Brian Rose approached what looked like being a century. 'Still beautiful to watch', says Robinson.

The small county ground, with its scorebox threatening to slide off the roof and its scoreboard glistening in the sun like a polished dining table, its two lines of trees, iron Jack White gates and peeling Edwardian decadence inside, is where Vivian Richards has grown from a week-end cricketer to the best—at his best—in the world. Somerset supporters have been privileged observers, witnessing the exasperating aberrations at the crease that punctuate lithe, peerless skills made for the poets. But there's the man as well as the cricketer. Seldom has another player been heard to make a snide or critical remark at Vivian's expense. A winking and envious throwaway about the lifestyle, maybe—but without a hint of malice.

He's a quiet charmer. Socially he prefers to stay in the corner of the room. Public chatter about the game and his own major contributions patently embarrasses him.

He isn't a great talker. Some find him positively taciturn. But he is good-natured, intelligent, gentle and courteous. He's slightly suspicious of newcomers and keeps his private views and intimacies well out of sight.

Cricketing friends end up with a uniform affection for the man without ever knowing too much about him.

Vivian is attractive to women. At the crease he moves with a languid sensuality. He bats with his sleeves buttoned at the wrists. The aubergine muscles show through his shirt. He walks with a slow, distinctive, rhythmic grace. He isn't especially tall but his shoulders are broad and he looks immensely strong— and paradoxically gentle—even in the way he lifts a glass of lager.

Women say he has a considerable animal magnetism. He probably enjoys their surreptitiously admiring glances. And in return he pays them compliments in that diffident way they find so appealing.

By comparison with more excitable West Indians he's positively phlegmatic. I've never seen him panic or, come to think of it, even rush. We have chatted, during the storms at the Weston-super-Mare cricket festival, when he came and sat in my car. It was parked 200 yards from the pavilion and he was next man in. Play had re-started long before he climbed out of the passenger's seat. Once or twice he wound down the window to ask someone in the nearby portable stand whether any more wickets had fallen. My mind was divided between Vivian's life story and the Somerset batting order on that August afternoon. His was entirely nostalgic, tripping back joyfully to schooldays at St John's.

I have talked to him between showers, innings, girl friends and occasionally headaches. Never once was I conscious, by any sign of temperament or swagger on his part, that I was with one of the greatest players the West Indies has produced.

Cricket without rushes of blood would be a barren battle. Of course Vivian has flashed that venomous bat when he shouldn't, and also given a dolly to mid wicket. Such errors of judgment, born of impatience and even over-confidence at times, make him privately angry.

He is, as Colin Atkinson reflects, more volatile than people think.

This, I accept, conflicts with the public face of him and the placid nature that I have emphasised. Yet the county president is right. As Somerset team-mates and Test match colleagues have witnessed, the Richards' eyes do sometimes flash.

That isolated incident at Harrogate, for which one or two spectators should feel eternally ashamed, is retold by Vivian in a later chapter—significantly without remorse.

The story that he tells in this book is one that illustrates just how minimally he has been affected by his hastily-achieved fame and the statistical grandeur that frequently seems almost incidental to his fundamental enjoyment.

He writes of Antigua's importance to him and gives some idea of the God-fearing family who helped to mould him.

It isn't a catalogue of cricketing feats, chronological and clinical. The game has never been like that to him. Aggregates hardly register with him. He enjoys belting a ball—and it's a bonus that he does it with such natural grace and ludicrous ease.

He's in no sense a complicated batsman with worries etched on his face as the ball cuts back wickedly off a green, capricious English wicket. He doesn't analyse every shot. His confidence is exceptional.

When he walks to the wicket at the county ground in Taunton, the farmers leave the market across the road just as they used to when Harold Gimblett was batting. His arrival at the crease in sporting arenas around the world brings an audible rustle of collective excitement unique in the current game.

The public, for reasons that are chemical as well as technical, markedly like or dislike top sportsmen. They all like Richards. While they marvel at his almost casual skills, they are never quite sure whether he is going to crack another record or be out. That, as part of the human condition, is the appeal of the man. No one knows how much longer Vivian Richards will go on playing or how soon the Packer acrimonies will be forgotten. With a cricketer of his instinctive make-up it's impossible to measure or guess at his future impact.

We have all seen him punishing disdainfully, almost comically, bowlers whose only sin is to pitch on a length. They are left shaking their heads and pondering disintegrating averages.

It was at a time like that at Weston that Somerset's former all-rounder Bill Andrews turned to the assembled company on the crowded boundary and said: 'This lovely bugger is going to score a thousand one of these days!'

Cricket, dare I suggest it, has come too easily to Richards. He has become a great player in no time at all. And I occasionally fear, knowing something of his temperament and personality, that he could even eventually become bored with the game.

He'd scoff at such a notion and I hope I'm proved wrong.

DAVID FOOT 1979

With My Family

Horatio Nelson arrived in Antigua one hundred and sixty eight years before me.

He came to my island because we had the best naval base in the Caribbean. This young, pallid, captain looked out to sea from the protective English Harbour and pondered how to sink the French fleet. Another preoccupation, so I've discovered, was an infatuation for a woman who was perhaps bored by her older husband.

Nelson, not always loved by West Indians, has still been something of a hero of mine—for his human weaknesses as much as his skills at sea. I quickly bracket him with more likely heroes.

If as a boy I visited Nelson's Dockyard to see where he slept and ate, I just as eagerly read every word written about Don Bradman and Gary Sobers. At school the three R's meant less to me than the three W's. Worrell, Weekes and Walcott ruled the West Indies in my happy, naive head. My father and his friends told me of these cricketers' greatness. The magnificent trio were to me the real makers of world history—more so than the statesmen and politicians. I'm not so sure that I'd got life out of perspective; if three sportsmen could fill a cluster of small islands with so much joy, firing the imagination of thousands of black schoolboys, their influence should never be underrated.

Travel is making me think. From a raw, carefree, rather lazy Antiguan boy I have gone by jet around the world in the last few years. The experience has come suddenly and unexpectedly to me. Distance now has a different meaning— and so have people.

But, oddly, as every day goes by—and every additional on drive continues to fill me with boyish excitement as it reaches the fence—I know that I belong more and more to Antigua. My roots are important to me. There is no happiness greater to me than to return to my parents in St John's, to sit in Albur's club where my brother Mervyn used to spin the music, or to jog along one of the island's powder-white beaches. I have plenty of choice with the beaches; we've got 365 of them.

Antigua, after all, is where I was born. It is where I used to watch my gentle and wizened grandmother pick the cotton in her backyard. It is where I played truant from school and sang oh-so-innocently in the Cathedral choir. It's where I once pinched mangoes with my friends and listened wide-eyed to the old islanders talking about the Jumbies—ghosts of the departed. It's where I had my first kiss and, still only fourteen, surrendered my virginity at carnival time as the fireworks banged. It's where I scored my first century, full of slogs and cheeky singles; and where later I was suspended for nearly two seasons by the Island cricket authorities for disputing a decision and causing a riot in the process.

I suspect I'm the only cricketer to have had three ducks in the same match. Only now can I begin to smile at the indiscretion committed on a dusty wicket as, with a youthful cussedness, I glared belligerently at the poor umpire.

That arrogant streak isn't really part of my nature. It wasn't the way that, looking back, I should have chosen to go into the Caribbean cricket record books. I'll return to the extraordinary and regrettable incident later in the book.

Antigua is only just over one hundred square miles. It has a beautiful coastline, nowadays dotted with yachts and other signs of a thriving tourist trade. Inland it's flat, dry, brown and not so beautiful. I'm still prejudiced enough to think it's the best of all the West Indian islands. It has its own trees and shrubs, its own smells—as when the sugar cane is burnt—its own customs and well-proportioned girls.

My birth in the local St John's hospital was on March 7, 1952. I'm sure my father, Malcolm Richards, a well-built and popular sportsman talented enough as a cricketer to play for Antigua as an allrounder, shared a few sporting intimacies with other visiting fathers in the hospital ward.

I have two half brothers, Donald and David, older than myself. A year after I was born, I had another brother, Mervyn, who now works as a clerk with the local airline. Donald is a qualified accountant; David is in a New York department store. We have remained a close and confiding family. I'm especially near to my parents although in the way of many West Indians they were strict with their children.

Occasionally when I was young and restless, I was apt to wander off and miss meals. 'But Mammy, I didn't know what the time was . . .'. My mother had her own unorthodox punishment for this. She would hide my trousers. I had only one pair and it meant that I was forced to stay indoors.

My parents insisted that I had both a decent education and the approved religious upbringing. As soon as I was old enough, they sent me to a small private school in St John's, run by Mrs Ross. The trouble was her nursery school didn't have much cricket on the curriculum.

From there I went to St John's Boys School. I can't say I was a particularly eager pupil and I'm grateful for the patience that masters like Mr Henry and Mr Mathias showed. I'd go off with a few of my friends—we used to 'scod' school. It wasn't that I hated lessons like some of the others; but there was always punishment if we arrived late in the morning and it seemed to make more sense to give it a miss altogether if we were running late.

I remember how much I enjoyed throwing stones—everyone did at that time. Kids can be cruel and we used to hurl stones at the lizards. We could be cruel with each other, too. Stone fights were popular on the days we didn't go to school. I suppose it might be argued that it taught us the value of agility. In my case, it certainly helped me to develop a good boundary arm for the future.

My next school was Antigua Grammar, where I arrived after passing the scholarship. I tried to buckle down. My best subjects were history and religious knowledge; I also enjoyed geography and science. I was slim but athletic.

Antiguans are easy-going and maybe not as lively and excitable as West Indians from some other islands. On the sports field I took on a new vigour and confidence. I was still much quieter than most of my friends. As soon as I picked up a bat, I seemed to take on a new personality.

The headmaster, Mr Loydston Jacobs, thought I had some promise and he encouraged me. So did the games master, Mr Reginald Samuels. Yet I didn't have much coaching. Perhaps if I had, I'd have 'holed out' less often and would have given my various Somerset skippers less chance of heart failure. But I certainly wouldn't have scored so many runs—or got them so quickly. And I'm sure I wouldn't have enjoyed my cricket half as much.

Coaching is a valuable but dangerous weapon as far as I can see. The good, natural coach builds on your strengths. If you do things in a bold, unorthodox way and get away with them, why be stripped of that skill and ability? Too many coaches have unwavering prejudices and too little imagination. They don't know the first thing about psychology.

I said I had limited coaching myself. That's perhaps less than fair to my father and to Pat Evanson, who lived opposite me at home in St John's. My father, who played soccer as well as cricket for the Island, was always passing on bits of advice to me in my early schooldays. He repeatedly told me not to hit everything of sight. 'D', as I called him, was annoyed when I was out to an impatient and bad shot.

Mr Evanson was once captain as well as wicket keeper for Antigua. Like my father, he was something of a celebrity. I felt proud that he lived so near me. He gave me my first bat when I was about twelve and I should say be inspired me as much as anyone.

'Hey, young Vivi, try to hit straight . . .'.

'Yes, Mr Evanson', I'd say. Advice from the island's former cricket captain was something to take seriously.

We were always talking sport at home, although I did most of the listening. I was still lacking in self-confidence. My father, home from his work at the local prison, would take me out in the yard for a knock-up. You couldn't rely on the bounce of the ball so I preferred the impromptu practice sessions up in the pastures not far from our house.

I seemed to be surrounded by cricketers. Donald opened the bowling for Antigua and also played for the Leeward Islands. I remember him slinging 'em down for Antigua on the day that Andy Roberts and I made our debuts. We must have had a useful pace attack. Andy was as quiet as I was. We went on to become firm friends and shared many a lunch-time hamburger, fruit punch and maybe rum and blackcurrant.

There's even a restaurant in the centre of St John's with a table reserved for the two of us. But I'll come to that later.

Brother David is not as sporting as Donald and is more interested in cars. Mervyn, however, like my father, has played both cricket and soccer for Antigua.

My parents' temperaments are different. 'D', whose mother was born in New York, is extrovert and quite excitable. He appears to be known by everyone. For a long time he was a warder at the prison and ended up, before his retirement, as deputy governor. He worked varying hours and when he was on the early shift my mother gave me his sandwiches to take to him for lunch. I was allowed in and usually had a word or two with some of the convicts. There weren't many hardened cons inside; mostly they were there, as far as I can remember, for thieving, assault and battery and a recurring record of petty offences. I know I used to recognise some of them from their days outside.

Partly because of his cricket, my father was a popular member of the prison staff. He used to assist with the preparation of the wicket on the St John's Recreation Ground, the venue for all the top matches. Often he brought a couple of 'trusty' prisoners with him to help with the work.

That is my father, then. My mother, also quite strictly Victorian in her attitudes, is a big woman, quiet and sensitive. Her ancestors came from Santo Domingo in the Dominican Republic. I also used to go to visit my grandmother and loved her very much. She was an enterprising and independent woman who grew cotton in her yard, picked it herself and then took it to the station in sacks to sell.

My immediate family remains a valuable influence on my life.

I always visit them, sadly only for a brief spell, at the end of the English cricket season. My father has now built an apartment on the top of his house in Drake Street; it's reserved for me when I go home and I'm touched by this kind of warmth.

The Anglican Church set many of the standards by which we lived. For several years I was an angelic soprano in the St John's Cathedral choir. Three times every Sunday I put on my dark blue cassock and white surplice and sang psalms and hymns, with one eye on the hymnal and the other, at least mentally, on the batting order for the next West Indian Test.

My days as a choirboy were apparently fairly tuneful. I was told I had a 'nice voice', although you'd never guess it as I hoarsely bellow a non-melodic 'Yes—er No—OK, a quick one!' in a tense Sunday League game.

I was in the choir when Queen Elizabeth of England came to the Cathedral. She passed within a few feet of my choirstall.

I remain a religious person to the delight of my parents. I pray every night before going to sleep; occasionally I pray for success on the field. Since coming to Somerset I have been godfather for a child of Peter and Eeva McCombe, personal friends of mine in Taunton, and for the baby of Ian Botham and his wife.

Like Horatio Nelson I have my share of human weaknesses. But I've gone through life with a fairly rigid personal code of conduct that includes, I like to think, courtesy and humility. I don't think I'll ever be in danger of getting swollen-headed.

All right, I know I'm beginning to sound like a paragon of virtue. So perhaps this is when I should redress the balance.

At school, as everyone keeps telling me at home, I could be very naughty. I got into fights and threw books in the classroom. I stole mangoes with my friend 'Tooko' Benjamin—not exactly the most dreadful of crimes—and by the age of fourteen, as I've said, I'd made the sexual breakthrough.

She was about the same age and went to a school nearby. The annual carnival was at its height and my head was full of steelband and calypso rhythms. The sideshows were blazing with neon lights. The beauty queens were gliding by on the floats. And we slipped away. We hardly met again.

I have been in love with the same girl now for a long time. We first met casually when I was only eight, and by the time I was seventeen we were going steady. Miriam Lewis, attractive and intelligent, used to attend the Girls' High School and had to come across to my grammar school for certain subjects. I'd walk her home during the lunch break and she would talk sport with a knowledge and quiet passion that left many of the boys standing. But her conversation was much wider than that.

In the early days I played in the same football team as her brothers and I was apt to pass them little messages to give Miriam. She supported most of the matches and would excitedly run on at the end if we had won. She would borrow my school tie and wave it from the pavilion during the game to let me know she was rooting for me. Soon she was pasting the first cuttings into what is now a massive scrap-book of my cricket career.

As a teenager, Miriam was as reserved as myself. When a local paper in Antigua published a picture of the two of us she burst into tears. She just couldn't cope with that kind of publicity. We smile about it now and she tells me, 'I've overcome that reserve and my present reaction would be completely different.'

But as I walked her home, hand-in-hand, from school a decade ago, her happy conversation gave me a lift. In the years that have followed, whatever the company and wherever the country, I've been bored by people who want to talk nothing but cricket. Maybe they think it's expected of them.

As Antigua is a small island—less than threequarters the size of Barbados and with a population of fewer than 70,000— many of the villages are almost within walking distance. In my schooldays, however I did some horse-riding. One pal of mine, Mickey Jarvis, whose father was the caretaker at the local botanical gardens and who owned some horses, used to invite me to go off with him. We used to ride bareback. Once I fell off and the horse trod on me but I survived with a few bruises.

Riding like that was a great way of seeing the island—the cane fields, coconut groves, the lovely red and white cedars and all those natural flowers like the yellow allamander and the red cordia.

And I'd look back fondly towards St John's, the capital on the hillside. Everywhere we rode we'd come up against remnants of the old sugar mills. I used to learn at school that in the 18th century there were nearly two hundred of them, including a lot of windmills.

Things have changed. Today there's only one main modern sugar factory, just outside St John's. New industries have taken the place of sugar and there is still sea-island cotton. But tourism outstrips the others.

You've only got to look at the flash new hotels and see the Americans and Europeans with their big cigars. You've only got to look along the coastline at the scores of handsome yachts.

Tourism has made my island wealthy. Some of my friends don't like the trend; they don't like to see the character of Antigua engulfed by outside business interests. I, too, have strong views about local culture and politics—views which I refuse to express even to my family—but I don't condemn the flourishing tourist trade. Antigua can't afford to do that.

The island has become more and more commercial in recent years, of course. That's why, when I go home, I prefer to do my occasional early-morning jogging and training at Fort James, not far from my home. I go as early as six o'clock in the morning and there aren't many about.

Certainly nothing like as crowded as the beach at Weston-super-Mare. . . .

But as schoolboys we didn't worry our heads about the big hotels that were going up alongside all the best beaches. Our only worry was that a greedy speculator might gobble up one of our cricket pitches.

Not that some of the parish grounds were good. In fact, you could say that a few were pretty dodgy.

When I played my first competitive cricket, I tried to bowl off-breaks rather than make runs. I once got 6–15 against Green Bay Government School. The ball was turning a mile without my really trying to spin it. But I wallowed in the congratulations and demonstrated to my envious teammates the current grip that I favoured.

In my St John's Boys School days I batted very much down the order. Then came Antigua Grammar School where gradually I was promoted to No. 5. I was usually in a hurry and had no obvious respect for the good bowler. Cricket was by this time becoming something of an obsession.

During the holidays brother Mervyn and I staged one-man Test matches in the yard or up in the pasture. When the ball hit the fence it was a six.

We did it properly, right down to a five-match series. 'You be Australia this week, Merv', I used to say. 'And I'll be the West Indies.'

The next week Mervyn was England. I always seemed to be the West Indies—Gary Sobers, Wes Hall and all. We kept detailed scores and played all day in that dusty yard. And we lost a few balls as the imaginary crowd cheered us on.

I became captain of the grammar school team and put myself at No. 3, the position I've kept for most of my professional career. I scored three centuries for them, although my first had been during my days at the St John's Boys School. It was on the King George ground in St John's, I remember, and I fancy I was dropped a few times!

The grammar school side was a strong one and we played in the first division of the Island's competition. I enjoyed flashing my bat and too often hit across the line to be caught at mid-wicket. Come to think of it, I still do.

When I left school at eighteen, my brother Donald suggested I join his club, St John's itself. The Antiguan medium-paced bowler Kenrick Isaac, who was captain of St John's helped to enrol me. I stayed for a couple of seasons, scored one century and did pretty well.

Another leading club in St John's was Rising Sun. They began to appeal to me more. One reason, I suspect, was that Andy Roberts was a member. He lived in the south of the island but we had met before and were friends. For a time we went round together like brothers. We made our debut for Antigua on the same day. Rising Sun had a good social life and the president, Mr Henry Lake, had a flair for organising.

I now come to the remarkable match that I played for Antigua against St Kitt's. I'll never forget it. Nor, I fear, will any of the 6,000 agitated spectators. Nor the rather more austere Island

25

cricket authorities who rapped me over the knuckles.

That day I felt in especially good nick. I had all the confidence, even cockiness of youth. I assured my friends that I'd be making a lot of runs. The St Kitt's bowlers didn't bother me. And then, almost as soon as I reached the wicket, I was given out. The umpire decided I'd been caught, bat and pad.

My behaviour was completely out of character. I hope I can excuse it up to a point in that it was my first zone match. I was tensed-up and wanted so much to do well.

Short-leg took the catch and the St Kitt's fielders screamed in united unison. They had no doubt about the fairness of the catch. Nor had the umpire. I knew I was not out. But I did a silly thing. I refused to go back to the pavilion. I stomped up and down. My temper got the better of me—I wasn't thinking straight.

I also said a few very pointed words to the umpire. Stalemate was reached and eventually I meandered off the pitch. I was still in a very bad mood.

I couldn't have guessed the reaction that would follow. I was a supposedly emerging young star in Antiguan cricket and everyone seemed to think I was going to score a ton. Fans came from all directions. They occupied the pitch. Demonstrators chanted angry words. Placards were hastily produced with this ultimatum:

'NO VIVI, NO PLAY'

Back in the pavilion all sorts of advice was being given me. I wasn't really in any state to receive it. 'Calm down, for Christ's sake!' someone said. I can't begin to analyse how I lost my head that day against St Kitt's.

Meanwhile, officials went into a long, anxious huddle. At last, after play had been held up for two hours, it was restarted—with I. V. A. Richards returning to the crease.

That was another mistake on my part. I went back because of pressure put on me to do so. The authorities saw that as the only way the match would continue. I was made to look a fool for the convenience of the local cricket establishment who had had the cheek to condemn me publicly for doing what they'd asked.

My father didn't go for me because I refused to walk—but because I allowed myself to be manipulated. A past captain of Antigua, Mr Leo Gore, whose opinions I respected so much, was also annoyed that this had happened.

I was young, immature and confused. I think I wanted to be out as quickly as possible. And I was—stumped without scoring.

The good nature of the crowd never really returned completely. The match was spoiled as a spectacle. Murmurings and heated argument went on through the four innings.

My mental approach was still bad. I was in no condition to make runs. And I was caught in the covers almost as soon as I'd taken guard in my second innings.

I wonder if any other cricketer can claim to have made three ducks in the same match. It's a bit of distinction I could have done without.

The authorities were far from pleased with the whole, noisy affair. They suspended me for two years from the end of the season, although I went on playing in the meantime. They didn't even tell me in the first place—I heard of my banning when I switched on the radio. Then the local newspapers, *The Star* and *The Workers Voice* took it up with headlines and editorials. Soon everyone on the island knew I was in so-called disgrace.

My cricket at all levels took a dive. Supporters who had put their faith in me began to wonder if it was misplaced. I struggled for runs and appeared to be losing my concentration. A succession of low scores didn't help my confidence—or my status.

Antiguan sports fans can be fickle, maybe with some justification. Some of them turned against me. They started booing and cat-calling me when I was at the wicket. They had obviously written me off as a promising young star.

Those cricket fans who went for me so viciously accepted that the Antiguan Cricket Association's rigid ruling put me in a position of public shame—and they weren't going to let me forget it. Some of the remarks were hurtful. A few of my newly-acquired critics even walked past my house in Drake Street, to shout insults and let my parents know what they thought of me. I stayed inside and was genuinely scared. The Leeward Islands banning jolted me. It was the first real lesson I had in the way cricket passions could run high—and the reverberations left my young head in a whirl. Just as well for me that Miriam was around to prove that I wasn't banned in love, at least. I still rather half-heartedly practised with my club and she would come along, probably after typing classes, piano practice or girl guides, for us to walk home together.

Since those callow, indiscreet days, I've learned to control flashes of temper. I don't often query umpire's decisions any more. It isn't always easy.

During the 1978 season, for instance, against Leicestershire at Taunton I was given out LBW to Ken Higgs by Bill Alley when I'd scored 99. I had some serious reservations about Bill's decision and so apparently had one or two of the Leicestershire players. I pulled off my gloves in spontaneous anger and banged my bat into the ground as I walked back to the pavilion. The crowd must have sensed that I was boiling. The lesson of self-control had been learnt, though, and five minutes later all was forgotten.

Of course, no-one likes being out on 99. . . .

Another overseas player in the West Country, Mike Procter, was out a few weeks earlier for 99 when playing for Gloucestershire at Cardiff. I understand that was also a doubtful decision. If I know Mike, he registered his personal protest with one or two lively bouncers later in the match.

I'm very much an admirer of this blond South African allrounder, like me a Packer player. Procter, shirt tail flying and streaming in on his long run-up, can be a fearsome sight for young, inexperienced professionals. Frustrated by defiant batsmen—especially against Somerset—he'll keep digging 'em in short. He can be an unfriendly bowler but never an unfriendly person. His politics are pretty liberal and I regret like many of my black friends that South African's race laws have kept him out of what would have been a distinguished Test match career. Kerry Packer belatedly allowed him to savour the international scene and earn a good wage for his considerable talents. Umpires' rulings balance themselves out over the years.

As I shall be telling you, on the day that Somerset's vice-chairman, Len Creed, made his decision to bring me back to England, I was stumped—and given not out! Everyone there, including Len Creed and maybe a kindly umpire, knew I was miles out of my ground.

That unhappy fiasco in the tense match with St Kitt's caused me to lose just a little of my appetite for cricket for a short time. But there was always football. Like my father and two of my brothers I had an aptitude for most ball games.

My position was centre half, or more a sort of sweeper as they would call it in Britain. By this time I was filling-out, acquiring muscles and broader shoulders. I fancied myself as a tackler and, although I played deep, I was apt to get a rush of blood to my head and take the ball more than half the length of the field. I captained my grammar school, even after I left. We played in the island's first division.

One of my rare goals from centre half sent me into raptures— yet never as much as when I'd gone down the wicket to hit the opposing quickie for a straight six.

At a time when I was showing promise again as a young cricketer, I was sent to England to attend Alf Gover's cricket school for six weeks. So was Andy Roberts.

'Don't let them change you too much, man', my friends said when they heard I was going.

But I'd been chosen by the coaching committee in Antigua and it seemed to be a wonderful chance and adventure.

England had always figured in my history lessons. It was the land of Nelson, Hood . . . and Hammond.

The night I was due to fly to London from Coolidge airport near St John's I was playing in an important soccer match against a leading side in the first division.

'No trouble, Vivi', my teammates assured me. 'You can do both.'

You'll have gathered that one of the characteristics of Antiguans is that they don't panic easily. Remember that the island was discovered by Colombus and named after a church in

Seville. The Spanish *mañana* approach has always appealed to me. We don't clutter our minds with unnecessary complications. When everyone else in the pavilion at Brisbane or Bath, for instance, is worrying about whether the wicket is going to last for three days, I don't reckon that need be my concern for the moment. I'll take it as it comes. Cricketers create needless anxieties for themselves.

But back to the football match on the night of my planned flight, with Andy Roberts, to Heathrow. We won the game 3–2. Then I washed, changed and was at the airport in half an hour.

'You've never moved so fast', some bloke shouted as I disappeared in a cloud of dust.

Anyone in cricket will tell you that no-one takes longer in the shower than me. Personal hygiene has always been a fetish of mine. I'm the last to leave the ground, refreshed and generously deodorised.

But that evening in Antigua I didn't have time for all the modern aids. I was piling into a car, tucking my shirt in and nervously gripping my small travelling bag. Andy was waiting, more anxious than I was.

We made our appointment with Mr Gover . . . just.

It was really the first and only official coaching that I ever had. I was taught to keep the bat and pad closer together. They didn't try to kill my natural aggression although I expect Mr Gover and his staff looked at one another and shook their heads a few times.

Just another raw West Indian, wet behind the ears, wanting to belt every ball out of sight.

I know I did many things wrong according to the cricket manuals. My feet weren't always quite right. I had too little of the required discipline.

'Look, Vivian', Mr Gover used to say, 'this is where we're going just a little wrong, when the ball is swinging away late . . .'.

He had a nice, helpful manner. I knew of his reputation as a brilliant coach. But it seemed to me an indoor cricket school at the start of a bitterly cold British winter was one hell of a long way from a sunny strip in St John's, where my volatile mates on the boundary advised me to whack every ball for six.

Above left The Richards family: father, grandmother with baby Mervyn, eldest brother Donald and myself.
Above right On confirmation day.
Below 'Not a bad sweeper, either!' Captain of the school soccer team against St. Mary's College in Trinidad.

I've never managed to acquire too much respect for bowlers. If I stop for long to ponder their well-known skills and the clever things they are supposed to be able to do off the seam or through the air, I'll never get round to making any runs at all.

I accept that this can underline a weakness in a batsman. Since coming to England I've worked tirelessly to show more control and discipline. The century I made against Warwickshire in the early rounds of the Gillette Cup in 1978 was perhaps one of my best innings. I refused to flash the bat.

On that afternoon at Taunton I grafted and watched the ball on to the bat until my eyes hurt. It won me the Man of the Match award—and I proved to myself that I could restrain myself in a way I didn't think possible.

At Mr Gover's indoor school, however, I wanted to show him that I knew how to hit the ball. Doug Livingstone, still playing for Hampshire at the time and living in London, came along I remember, to give some help and encouragement.

The six weeks in England weren't exactly the height of riotous living for two shy young Antiguans who had hardly been away from home before.

We stayed, to start with, at a guest house in Putney. Suddenly we felt very lonely and missed our friends. Each day we went on the tube to the cricket school. Although our visit had been funded from home by the Voluntary Coaching Committee, we had little spare cash in our pockets. We went to the movies a few times and had a look inside a few London pubs. Once Andy and I went to see Arsenal play Leeds United at Highbury. That, in fact, was one of the highlights of our stay in England.

Andy had a sister who lived at Hackney. We moved there from our guest house and felt more at home. We sat glued to the television set in the evenings.

It was bitterly cold. I turned up alone one day at Mr Gover's school. And I had to be honest when I was asked about Andy's whereabouts.

'The cold, Mr Gover, it's the cold. Man, Andy is staying in bed all day today.' It seemed like the best place, under those blankets.

* * *

32

I'd left school a year or so before this with a modest but adequate academic record. Maybe I should have worked harder. My father was pushing me, spelling out the financial advantages of a decent career.

I'd been a popular kid at school—for my sport, I imagine, rather than my lessons. I read quite a lot, mainly about my cricketing idols. It never really entered my head that I might make a living myself from the game. My centuries—and tendency to hit sixes—had made me a bit of a local talking point. My family usually kept me down to earth. They weren't going to have any show-off about the house.

Miriam, my constant girl friend, refused to feed my ego. She seemed to me the cleverest girl in St John's and if she told me I'd let the side down with one wild, irresponsible swing, I dutifully believed her.

In the years that followed I became more self-critical as a result.

My first job after leaving school had been at D'Arcy's Bar and Restaurant in St John's. The late owner, D'Arcy Williams, took a kindly interest in me. He'd been, in effect, my first sponsor. He kitted me out in new whites, gloves and pads. He gave me a new bat—and made me feel like a real cricketer.

'Would you like a job, young Vivi?' he asked one day. 'The tips are very good.'

And so they were. Mr Williams ran one of the biggest and most popular restaurants in the area—and now he had a new waiter.

Once I spilled the drinks when someone bumped into me. But I got the hang of gliding between the tables, calculating the tips by the size of the customer's cigar.

Many of the people who came into the restaurant and bar were Americans. I found that with my quiet and I hope courteous manner and efficiency with the orders I could knock up 60 dollars a week on tips alone.

It wasn't difficult for a waiter to get a date with one of the attractive American or Canadian ladies who came in for a meal or a drink. This was particularly true at carnival time. They'd come to Antigua to enjoy themselves and, if they were

33

unattached, to have a run-round. A surprising number didn't seem to have any immediate ties. The local boys could quickly weigh-up the pretty visitors.

Stray liaisons weren't uncommon, of course, when the carnival was in full, exotic swing.

My days as a waiter saved my father's pocket. When I wasn't working he used to be very generous with my pocket money. My older brother also helped out at times. And for quite a lot of the time I wasn't working at all. I didn't have any guilt feelings about this and assumed that some career would eventually turn up. I'm afraid I wasn't in too much of a hurry for this to happen. Thinking back, my parents were probably getting slightly worried. My father had plans for me to study electrical engineering and was actually on the point of sending me off to New York—where we had a number of relatives—when I suddenly discovered I had the chance of a possible cricket career in England.

Manual work never filled me with much enthusiasm.

Later, in my first year at Bath waiting to get my chance for Somerset, they kept me occupied as an assistant groundsman.

'It's not for you, is it, Viv?', the club chairman used to say. 'You'll never get blisters on your hands!'

A cousin of mine, Bob Daniel, has an engineering business in Antigua. There were times when I'd go out and help him, trying my hand as a mechanic, repairing cars and bulldozers.

This arrangement, I remember, had its snags. The work occasionally took us well into the country and if I was stranded miles from St John's on a Saturday morning, there could be anxieties ahead for my cricket club.

More than once I arrived late at the ground, to be greeted by reprimanding looks from the officials. Worse, my hands were still covered in oil, some of which had smeared on to my flannels.

I must have been less conscious of my appearance in those days. The thought of those oily whites makes me cringe. And smile at the same time.

I'm not sure how highly cousin Bob rated me as an apprentice mechanic. Antigua C.C., I do know, rated me a lousy timekeeper.

I've improved my sense of punctuality since then, not having to hitch a lift in a van to the ground any longer. As for my appearance nowadays, I'm supposed to be, according to my teammates either in England or Australia, one of the sharper dressers in the game. That doesn't, I hope, make me sound like a peacock. I've never been as vain as all that. I do enjoy, though, being neat and tidy . . . and trendy.

For some time I may not have had a regular job. But the appeal of living in St John's was obvious. Who could better my mother's cooking?

Some of the neighbours in Drake Street used to say: 'Gratel, you prepare the best pepperpot for miles.'

And so she did. Also the best pancakes. The best banana fritters. The best seasoned rice. . . .

My mother was always baking. Every time I go home I put on weight. And I love her for it.

Who wanted to jet off to New York and join the rat-race when life could be lived at Antigua's leisured pace? I went to New York several times to visit relatives and couldn't wait to return home. America's so-called sophistication and pace were altogether too much for me. My father's mother was American and I think it may have been planned for me to end up there. If I'd gone off in 1973 to study electrical engineering, the break would have been made for ever. Unless, as I fancy would have happened, the pull of calypso cricket had become too great.

Antigua was right for me. My temperament belonged there—in the island where the taxi drivers keep their fares waiting while they chat to their friends and check the latest cricket score; where dusty inland roads aren't bedevilled with double yellow lines and hooting horns; where the crack of a six is as sweet as the Cathedral bell.

I had, after all, come to know so many of the genuine characters. Cricketers like Tyrone 'Pacer' Williams and Hilson Phillip.

'Pacer' was one of the Antiguan bowlers when I was playing for the island. He wasn't exactly short of self-confidence. In one zone match, he ran up to bowl to the opposing captain. There was no doubt in 'Pacer's' mind—this skipper was one of the most conceited players on the scene at the time. He needed to be put in his place.

The delivery contained all of 'Pacer's' cunning. It knocked all three stumps over. But the jubilant bowler wasn't content with that. Deliberately he rolled the ball to the dismissed batsman and said, 'Go and put that in your freezer, man!'

From slip I watched the little confrontation and roared with laughter. 'Pacer' never had a sweeter triumph.

As for Hilson, he wouldn't stop talking. He played for St John's and Antigua and was nearly as good a talker as he was a cricketer. His particular skill, it appeared to me, was to be able to distract the opposition. We have a few 'talkers' in county and Test cricket—but none was in the Phillip class.

I was batting against St Kitt's and Hilson was at the other end. The bowler took a long run and had plenty of fire. He could make them rear up.

Just as he was about to bowl to me, Hilson started his monologue. 'You think you came here to bowl, why you couldn't even drink milk!'

His expressions were crazy and made you double-up. They were also the best example of good-natured gamesmanship on the island. The bowler, distracted by such an unexpected and untimely insult, lost his length. I started hitting a few boundaries.

All is fair on a sunny Antiguan afternoon.

Who wanted to go off to New York and miss all this?

From the early schooldays when I rode off on my bike or horseback with friends like 'Tooko' Benjamin, Mickey Jarvis, 'Beeket' Michael and 'Tohijo' Carbon, to explore those parts of Antigua that I couldn't see from my home in St John's, I was a sucker for this small, oval island.

I occasionally went as far as English Harbour and Nelson's Dockyard and imagined the days when fine ships were refitted and Nelson was bothered by mosquitoes and his own emotions.

St John's, some would say, isn't the most beautiful capital in the West Indies. But you won't hear me saying a bad word about it. It's built on a hillside and is much greener than some of the flat, dry, brown land you see as you move from the coast. The

36

Cathedral, where I sang until my voice began to break, stands out. The original building was destroyed by an earthquake in 1843; when it was erected again five years later they took precautions in case there were more tremors.

You'll find plenty of modern buildings like the bank where Miriam works, and the supermarkets. The gift shops are full of miniature steel bandsmen and limbo dancers. You can buy Irish linen, Swiss watches, English china, French perfume—as you can in any gift shop in nearly any country.

If the locals want to buy rum they don't go to the big hotels. Then buy it at their own stores where it's cheap and potent. They like the excuse for a party. The carnival which starts the week before the first Monday in August is a fantastic event and I'm sad that I've missed it so much in recent years because of my cricket around the world. We get visitors from the neighbouring islands. Tourists gaze wide-eyed at the spectacle. The big day is the Jouvert Jump-Up. And you can say that again. We're celebrating emancipation in 1834; but, in effect, we're celebrating almost anything we care to drink or dance to. The girls, red-lipped and shapely, compete for the beauty queen title and the tableaux go by in a long procession. And none of us knew there were so many steel bands around.

I've known up to 140 musicians in one steel band. The throbbing atmosphere makes you high. Once I had some lessons and nervously joined a band. It was an added kick to take part in the carnival procession that way.

*   *   *

'It's time you were on your way, Vivi. I'm sending you to New York. That's where you'll get some proper training for a career'.

My father's advice more than once put an end to my reveries about Antigua.

And it began to make sense. I'd achieved the obvious cricketing ambitions by 22 years old—to play for my island and the Leeward Islands, progressing to Combined Islands in the Shell Shield tournament. The Leewards and Windwards

37

combine to play against Jamaica, Barbados, Trinidad and Guyana.

You don't make any money turning out regularly for Rising Sun, of course. Some cricketers had gone off to England to play—and get paid for it. Sir Gary Sobers, whom I watched swinging his bat so gracefully in Antigua on his visits, was just one of an increasing number.

He's a Barbadian and Barbardos was, on that level, one of my favourite cricket islands. I'd met Hallam Moseley when he first returned home to play Shell Shield matches after a season with Somerset. Hallam seemed to be enjoying himself. We had a chat when I played against him for Combined Islands. I then had absolutely no thoughts of coming to England myself.

The notion that I might one day be sharing a hotel room with Hallam, as Somerset played their first class fixtures around England and Wales, was unthinkable to me.

I had Mr Charlie Henry to thank for letting me see my first Test in Barbados. He was a successful businessman in Antigua who had taken an interest in my progress as a teenager. Mr Henry organised a trip for young cricketers to go to Barbados to see the West Indies play New Zealand at Bridgetown.

I couldn't begin to tell you what kind of impact that match had on me, soon after I'd left school. For one thing, I'd never seen such a crowd before. They were making a continuous rhythmic din long before the match was due to begin. My stomach was turning over and I wasn't even playing.

From all sides of the ground the Caribbean banter was going on. Everyone was in high spirits. Improvised steel bands were starting up all around me. I lived through the heady experience of a score of brilliant centuries. And the match hadn't even started.

In fact, Gary Sobers and Charlie Davis both got hundreds. It was wonderful stuff, filling me with as much joy as when later I hit a Test double century.

Afterwards in the dressing room I was introduced to Mr Sobers. It was a brief, happy moment.

I was tongue-tied.

The Jamaican Lawrence Rowe was another idol of mine. At that same Bridgetown Test match he actually gave me his gloves as a keepsake. Imagine what that meant to one lad from Antigua.

I treasured those gloves as if they were jewels. Back in Drake Street I bought an aerosol and sprayed the name YAGGA across our galvanized fence. That was Lawrence Rowe's nickname.

People used to see the name on the fence and ask me to explain it. And I would tell them about the pair of Test match gloves I had up in my bedroom.

It wasn't the only treasure in my bedroom. That was where I kept my bat. I used to run my hand along it when I woke up in the morning. I'm telling you, silly as it sounds, that I was in love with that first bat of mine.

But now here was my father, big Malcolm Richards, deputy prison governor, successful Antiguan cricketer and above all realist, deciding it was time I was given some down-to-earth professional guidance.

He'd heard there was a chance for me to go to Lancashire and play some league cricket for Oldham. What did Oldham mean back in St John's? They weren't even a county side.

'Sort yourself out, Vivi. They don't play cricket in New York. But they'll put you on your feet. You can't go on for ever without a career.'

Miriam, too, was thinking it was about time I looked beyond carefree weekend cricket. My mother, in her quiet way, was also worrying a bit about me.

I was in a spot of confusion for the first time. I'd been nurtured on Worrell, Weekes and Walcott; then I'd watched Sobers, Clive Lloyd and Rohan Kanhai. And there was this engaging guy called Hallam Moseley beaming and saying life was great in Stogumber and Stoke St Gregory!

But I sensed that New York was winning. I started collecting my things together and packing my case. I even began saying goodbye to some of my Saturday night party friends. I'd spilled my last drink and taken my last generous tip for gliding between the tables at D'Arcy's.

There was a provisional place at night school in New York waiting for me. I was just about to buy my air ticket. And then I had a visitor. In some ways he was just another tourist. He was on holiday with his wife.

With Lansdown

Len Creed was my idea of an English farmer. He had broad shoulders, a ruddy complexion and an accent that, to my mind, belonged to the countryside.

In fact, as I later discovered, he came from the Somerset village of Evercreech where his father was a farmer.

Mr Creed was at that time the vice-chairman of Somerset. He was also a successful bookmaker in Bath where in the English summer months he had, for some years, kept one ear on the 'blower'—for the latest starting prices—and the other on anyone prepared to pass on the current county score.

I didn't even know where Somerset was, apart from the fact it was Hallam Moseley's new home.

To even things out Antigua meant very little to Mr Creed. 'I knew it was one of those West Indian Islands but I couldn't even pronounce the bloody place properly', he joked afterwards.

The Somerset vice-chairman and his wife Betty had come to the West Indies with an ambitious touring club side called Mendip Acorns, run by a chap called Norman Teer who was a bit of an organising genius. I don't know how they managed it but their tours seemed to take them halfway round the world. They also had the knack of persuading one or two successful county players to join them.

This particular year the party included Kent's Derek Underwood, Glamorgan's Alan Jones, Gloucestershire's Sadiq Mohammed and a slightly overweight and talented cricketer Richard Cooper who, although still young, had in his time played for Somerset. Most of them had gone for the sun and a few carefree games of cricket. Mr Creed had, unknown to the other members of the Somerset committee, apparently gone to look for a player . . . me.

In his wallet he carried a small creased and thumbed cutting from 'The Cricketer'. It simply said that Colin Cowdrey, who had gone the previous year to the West Indies, had been asked if he had spotted any useful young players.

'There was a chap called Vivian Richards who looked promising.'

Just that, more or less. But Mr Creed cut it out when he should have been checking the runners for the 2.30. And now he wanted to see for himself.

He was, as I learned, an independent bloke. He was used to making snap decisions and risking hundreds of pounds on a single race. Now he was prepared, entirely off his own bat, to test his judgment again.

I've heard the story many times since. The Mendip Acorns, mostly easy-going, Saturday-afternoon West Country types, with a few Welsh and Kentish accents interspersed, arrived in early April.

Mr Creed was in a single-minded mood. He climbed out of the plane at Coolidge Airport and into a taxi. The driver was 'Willie', a well-known character on the Island.

'Ever heard of a chap called Vivian Richards?'

You couldn't get quicker to the point than that. Willie looked back at his fare and beamed.

'Yes, sir—he's the best cricketer on the Island.'

On the short journey from the airport to the Blue Waters Hotel, Willie extolled my virtues. He was clearly among my fans, not one of those fickle mates who gave me the bird after I was suspended.

'If you want, sir, I'll take you to meet one of his friends.'

'Great—put your foot down, Willie', said Mr Creed, already on Christian-name terms with his taxi driver.

There was hardly anyone around in the hotel except two barmen polishing the glasses. It was mid-day and very hot.

Willie introduced Mr Creed to one of them, who must have been impressed when this big, jolly newcomer announced he was the vice-chairman of a county club in England.

42

'Vivian, sir? Would you like to have a word with him? I can arrange it.'

Len Creed, impatiently gulping down his first drink of the day—and mopping his brow at the same time—didn't have time to say yes.

'And would you like to meet Andy Roberts, his friend, as well?'

The English visitor admitted to me afterwards that he wanted to say, 'And who the hell is Andy Roberts?'

Andy, of course, wasn't known in England then although he was on the point of flying over to qualify for Hampshire.

Mr Creed was too polite to show his ignorance about the best pace bowler in Antigua and soon to prove one of the fastest in the world.

'How long?'

'Leave it to us.'

Willie was given the instructions and off he went. I hope he didn't lose too many taxi fares in the meanwhile. But that's the joy of living and working in Antigua. We don't get things out of perspective. Cricket usually comes first.

And Willie was back in the hour. He had two shy young West Indians with him, Andy and myself. There was a third passenger in the taxi, Brann Jacobs, a local businessman who acted as our adviser on such mind-bending matters.

I took a liking to Mr Creed at once, not just because he bought the first round of drinks!

I'd been practising with my club side, Rising Sun C.C., when Willie rushed up to me.

'Hey, Vivi. Get into this taxi. I've got the vice chairman of a big club in England waiting to see you up at the Blue Waters Hotel.'

While we had our drinks, Brann and Mr Creed did most of the talking. Mr Creed had a warm manner which I liked. He laughed a lot. And he proudly pulled out his cutting from 'The Cricketer'.

He seemed at bit taken back when Brann Jacobs said Andy was already booked for Hampshire. He was even more surprised when he learned that I had the chance to go to Oldham to play in the Lancashire League.

43

'I was afraid you were on the way towards becoming a Lancashire player and that I'd got to you too late', he told me later.

I reassured him. They already had Clive Lloyd and they wouldn't want an unknown who hadn't, in honesty, got much further than the President's XI at home.

In that hotel lounge, Andy and I looked at each other—and dreamed of a career away from Rising Sun, the St John's club, where we tried to win the matches on our own in the scorching hot afternoons and enjoyed, almost as much, the parties afterwards.

Mr Creed was, I knew, a successful bookmaker. He would have been even better as a salesman.

'Now Lancashire is all right, Vivian. But, I mean, take the weather.'

I began to think of monsoons or something.

'They have all this rain in Lancashire. Now . . . the West Country! That's different. Best weather in the whole of England. Sunshine just like Antigua', he said. And then added almost apologetically I thought, '. . . At least, some of the time . . .'.

He went on, 'There're lovely people in the North Country, of course. They'd make you very welcome. But so would we. I was born in Somerset and wouldn't live anywhere else'.

The next day Mendip Acorns were playing Antigua. Somerset's vice chairman was going to be watching. We had another round of drinks in the Blue Waters Hotel and then we shook hands.

I'd barely opened my mouth. But weeks later Mr Creed told me I'd impressed him by my 'pleasant manner, and impeccable appearance'. Little did he know I'd come straight from cricket practice.

'See you tomorrow then, Vivian. Get a few runs.'

I murmured that I'd try. How about Moseley and Richards for Somerset, I asked myself in bed that night? The more I thought about it, the more I liked the idea. I slept hardly at all.

Danny Livingstone, the former Hampshire player was captaining Antigua against Mendip Acorns. He, in fact, had met

Len Creed before. They shared an interest in antiques and Danny had stayed at the Creed home in Bath. I discovered later that Mr Creed contacted Danny and asked him what he thought of me as a cricketer. 'He'll do all right in England', was the kind reply.

The game against the touring club side from the West Country on the Recreation Ground at St John's was the most important, arguably, in my whole career. It was also perhaps the most farcical.

I suspect it was the fact that I was being watched. Everyone on the ground seemed to know. Most of them wanted me to do well. A few hoped that I would fail so that I would stay in Antigua and continue playing for Rising Sun—for nothing more than a cool beer and a laugh afterwards. If I wanted to impress the man from England, I didn't go about it the right way. I couldn't decide whether to play back or forward; whether to show-off my natural free swinging game or to prove that I could play down the line like Mr Gover had once demonstrated.

With a rush of blood I took an almighty swish with the intention of sending the ball not only into the sea but probably into the meadows of Somerset as well. I missed the ball by a mile and was stumped. I must have been more than a foot out of my ground.

The Acorns' wicket-keeper screamed his appeal and looked at 'Nookie' the umpire at square-leg. There was a brief pause. 'Not out!'

Lovely 'Nookie', doing his bit for Vivian Richards's future career. . . .

I think the fielders were bemused. I'm not sure they will ever again say a good word for the standard of umpiring in Antigua.

But I was still there, Len Creed was grinning broadly and the spectators were calling for a six.

I went on to make 30 or so runs. Then I was caught behind and everyone on the ground heard the snick. There couldn't be another let-off. I walked very slowly back to the pavilion and wondered if I'd blown it.

Ironically it wasn't my batting that clinched my coming to Somerset. I was fielding in the covers that day and I ran out one

of the Mendip Acorns' batsmen with a sharp, under-arm throw.
As the stumps were hit, Mr Creed turned to Mr Louis
Powell, a former Somerset committee man who was standing
next to him.
'I'm going to have him, Louis. I'm taking Vivian back to
Somerset with me and I'm chancing my arm.'
He was doing that right enough. The more I thought about it,
the more I accepted that my record was a modest one. Centuries
at school-boy level in Antigua were one thing; playing for a
leading county in England was another. Suddenly those
matches for Antigua itself, the Leeward Islands, Combined
Islands and the President's XI were not quite as world-
shattering as I'd imagined they were at the time.
For the rest of his stay in the West Indies, Mr Creed kept in
touch with me. He wrote and phoned from St Lucia and
Grenada; he corresponded with Brann Jacobs and Danny
Livingstone.
It was agreed that I should go to England. The arrangement
was based on trust.
'You will come', Mr Creed told me 'and I'll make sure you
have sufficient money to carry you through the coming season.
If you aren't good enough, I'll make myself responsible for
putting you on the plane again in September. It won't cost you a
penny.'
'And who will I play for? I know I can't walk into the
Somerset team.'
'I'm the chairman of a very old-established club called
Lansdown, in Bath. You'll love the lads there. And after a year,
I'm banking on your becoming a Somerset player.'
It seemed as though we were both taking a chance, although I
appreciated the generosity and faith shown in me.
As if to reassure me, my new guardian said: 'Don't worry,
Vivian, I'll make certain you have something to eat and drink all
the time you're in England.'
Unfortunately we understandably ran into difficulties with
the flight. Mr Creed couldn't get me on the same plane as
himself. But after a lot of frantic running around, I was booked
on a flight which was due to arrive in London the same day as the
returning Acorns.

At Heathrow, Mr Creed and Richard Cooper waited for two hours. And then the pantomime started. I'd arrived and didn't have a work permit.

The immigration people weren't very impressed with my rather weak story that I'd come to England to play for a club called Lansdown. They wanted to know if I was being paid for it. I became more and more anxious and confused.

The authorities went into a huddle and put me on a bench to wait. It was the bench, I assumed, where they usually direct you before sending you home on the next available flight.

Cricket seemed a long way away. I was tired and hungry—and just wanted to get back to my parents or to my friends in one of the little friendly St John's bars where work permits were possibly never discussed.

'Call Mr Creed', I eventually blurted out. 'He'll explain'.

He was waiting downstairs, wondering what the hell was going on.

They sent for him and he arrived to see me holding my head in my hands. He said I looked in a dreadful state.

'Don't panic', he told me with what must have been more bravado than confidence. 'I'll ring the Home Secretary'.

He didn't need to go quite to that extent. With gambler's luck, he found an immigration official who had both cricketing and West Country connections. 'Give me half an hour and I'll try to fix something', he said.

He fiddled his way through the red-tape and soon we were in Richard Cooper's car speeding west. I slept in the back as we headed along the M4 towards Bath. My first temporary home was with Mr Creed and his wife.

I was still tired but remember thinking how green everything looked—the back gardens full of spring vegetables, the parks and flowers around this attractive city. I'd never seen a place remotely like this before. But my early impressions were cut short. 'Come in, Vivian. I'm taking you round to the Lansdown club. Try a drop of English beer and meet the lads.'

His home was only 200 yards from the ground. They used to joke it was because he could get home safely after a few whiskies.

In the clubhouse I was being offered a drink on all sides. Mr

Creed had been in touch with his son while away and everyone seemed to know that, without a word to the Somerset committee, the vice chairman had forked out to bring me to England with the hope that I'd make the grade.

The air fare was reimbursed, of course. But it was a remarkable thing for a committee man to do.

It didn't look as though Lansdown would be able to find out that coming Saturday. All the teams had been selected.

'We'll get you a game with someone else in Bath for one week', I was told.

But the next day someone dropped out of the 2nd XI, due to play away at somewhere called Weston-super-Mare. And that was where I made my English debut on April 26th, 1973.

They gave me a lift to the ground and I remained tight-lipped and nervous. The team was an interesting collection—old and young, fat and thin. Nothing like a typical black side at home. But they were friendly, chatting all the time while I changed, to make me relaxed.

Weston batted first and I was horrified by the wicket. It was softer than I'd ever seen before, a pudding. Remember I'd just come from the bone-hard strips of Antigua.

Back in the pavilion at Lansdown that evening, I eavesdropped on the conversation between Len Creed and Alan King who had opened the batting with me. Lansdown's chairman couldn't wait to hear about his protégé.

'Well, then, Alan, what happened?'

'You've got a good 'un there, Len.'

'But what happened?'

'We bowled Weston-super-Mare out for 95. Then I went in with young Vivian. I got 29 and he got the rest. He even finished the game off with two sixes.'

It wasn't quite as carefree as that sounds. I didn't know what to make of that spongy wicket. So I took a good, hard look at it before cutting loose.

They put me into the Lansdown first team after that. But there are other things to life besides cricket.

Bath is a sedate city where the tourists come in the summer to take pictures of the Abbey or visit the Roman Baths. I couldn't get over the lovely architecture of the place. We've got some pretty good buildings at home like the mid-18th century Court House or Clarence House which was built for Prince William Henry, Duke of Clarence, and where various members of the British Royal Family have stayed since the war. But those Georgian crescents at Bath were wonderful. I used to walk along them and wonder what they were like inside. Accommodation was, in fact, quite a problem for me in my early days at Bath. I obviously couldn't stay indefinitely with Mr Creed.

There's quite a big black community in Bath, mainly Barbadian. Terry Harding, an umpire with Lansdown for 24 years, had the job apparently of finding me digs. And he says it wasn't too easy at first.

Hallam Moseley, who had also played for Lansdown while qualifying for Somerset, was a Barbadian. There was no difficulty finding him rooms—and no lack of vocal support when he was playing.

I must say at once that I was never conscious of any discrimination against me from the Barbadians because I was Antiguan. My time in Bath was always friendly. But Terry Harding says that when he first went to the Russell Street area of Bath to try to find a room for me, my Antiguan background went slightly against me. It quickly changed, in any case, when I became known locally.

Inter-island rivalry in the West Indies is a fact of life although it has never bothered me. I suppose it was natural that the people from Barbados in Bath should want to stay together and be just a little suspicious of an unknown newcomer from Antigua.

In any case I was found a small room in Russell Street. The house seemed to be full of steel drums—so I should have felt at home.

There were also plans for me at one time to stay at the Y.M.C.A., in Bath. . . . Maybe my Lansdown friends were influenced by my strict Anglican background!

Alas it lasted for only one night—or, in fact, less than that. One of my Lansdown mates, Alan Bees—a player member for more than 40 years, he claims—saw me safely booked in. Then he and his friends took me off to Grant's nightclub which, I suppose, was the peak of sophisticated late-night living in those days.

About midnight I began to feel like Cinderella. I'd been in a few strange beds in my time but the Y.M.C.A. was different. I wondered if there was a curfew.

'I think I'd better be off', I said, sinking my lager.

At 12.30 a.m. my Lansdown team-mates were surprised to see me back. I was in a bit of a state.

'I can't get in. All the doors and windows are locked. What the hell am I going to do?'

My first impressions of England weren't quite what I'd expected. I was nearly sent back from Heathrow on the next plane . . . and here I was out on the streets of Bath in the early hours of the morning without a bed for the night. Alan Bees, not for the only time during my eventful and adventurous period with Lansdown, came to the rescue. He put me up for the night.

I had a more peaceful sleep at his home than when later the two of us went out for a late night and got separated. I returned to his home at 3 a.m. but noticed that his car was still missing. Ever loyal to a mate—we were supposed to be together—I went off again. In the meantime Alan came back and assumed I was already asleep. He went in, locked the door and bolted it on the inside and crept up to bed. At 6 o'clock I arrived back again, tired but still loyal. I looked under the mat and tried the lock. No luck. Confused by a ploy that had gone wrong, I rang the door bell.

Mrs Bees jumped out of bed and came downstairs to open the door. Unthinking, I blurted out: 'Is Alan home yet?' That took some explaining.

It was a strange world in Bath. I missed the sun and the brown, dusty Antiguan landscape that was part of me. I missed the calypso music and the late-night gossip about Shell Shield matches and boastful sexual claims and the white wooden houses and idle shop-gazing in St John's High Street. And all those beaches where you could jog or laze or flirt. And the grinning taxi drivers who were never in too much hurry to pull alongside you and offer an assessment of your last six over extra cover. And I missed Miriam.

For some weeks after I arrived in Bath I was lost. The weather was cold and uninviting. And not even those lovely terraces in Bath look good when the sun isn't shining. Apart from all that, there was something lacking. Remember I was in my early 20s, a virile black athlete.

Finding girl friends in a place like Bath, which is dominated by an Abbey and middle-aged, middle-class people understandably set in their ways, wasn't easy. There weren't so many eligible girls of my age group around as far as I could see. Most of those who came to the Lansdown club already had their boy friends or husbands. And I was, after all, a young black man among a lot of white people.

I think there was a touch of desperation in the way I at last found the courage to approach Mr Creed. He'd been taking a fatherly interest in me and seemed the right person to offer a little guidance on matters personal as well as cricketing.

I chose the right moment when we were alone. He knew I wanted to say something to him but couldn't find the right words.

'What is it, Vivian?'

'Well, sir, it's—well—yes, you know, I've been in this country for more than six weeks now and . . .'

'And what, Vivian?'

'I haven't met a lady, you know. Em-can you do anything for me?'

I don't know what the Lansdown chairman thought. He'd already paid for my air fare from Antigua and was trying to make me into a cricket star. He'd even let me stay at his nice home for a few days.

We have laughed about it many times since. I suppose I thought he had all the right connections. In fact, he didn't let me down.

Over a drink in the Lansdown Club, Mr Creed later whispered jokingly to me: 'I know I'm vice chairman of Somerset but I didn't know that pimping was part of my job!'

* * *

Clearly I wasn't yet a county player and there was no

guarantee that I would be. Who was going to pay for me to stay in England? At least I needed enough to buy my round of drinks—I always insisted on that.

The club chairman had worked that out, too. He made me assistant groundsman at Lansdown under John Hayward. I'm not sure I was such an advantage to have around. I was shown how to start the mower and when to roll the square. Each day I reported dutifully for my job. I wasn't in love with it—and I expect it showed. I used to look at my hands and see the blisters coming. Cricket to me was walking down the wicket with a swinging bat—not a heavy roller.

I was paid £1 a day for my labours and probably it came out of Mr Creed's own pocket. Occasionally my new teammates would ask: 'What's it going to play like on Saturday, Viv?' I'd look up at the heavy skies and say knowledgeably: 'The sun's on the way after the rain. So just right for your leggers . . .'. My short, untaxing apprenticeship as a cricket groundsman was nothing more than a convenient stopgap.

During the time that I cut the square—under John Hayward's critical but kindly eye—I acquired a liking for local girls, Guinness and jazz music. But, for the time being, back to my cricket.

After that opening knock on the spongy Weston-super-Mare wicket I was considered ready for the first team at Lansdown. I was accepted as a bit of a cricketer. The lads in the bar approved of me. 'You've brought back a useful one here, Len' they used to say.

'Course I bloody have', he'd replied. 'Don't you trust my judgment?'

One member of the side at that time was 'Shandy' Perera, from Ceylon. He was a talented all-rounder who usually opened the bowling. I took a liking to him from the start. He offered me sensible advice about batting on English club wickets. It was no good for me to wait all the time with the intention of playing off the back foot as I did with most of my success at home. I needed to begin striking the ball off the front, he told me.

After every game at Lansdown, 'Shandy' and I would discuss where, if I was recklessly out, I'd gone wrong. All through my

Len Creed—the man who discovered me.

career it was people like 'Shandy', my father and Pat Evanson, whose helpful words in my ear did so much to make me into a Test cricketer. They've no idea how grateful I am to them.

Lansdown is a club which comes alive after the games on Saturday. All three elevens converge on the pavilion. The various scores are put up to the accompaniment of whoops of delight or groans. When we were playing away, we always made a point of getting back to our own club for what we hoped would be the congratulations of the other members. Then, after a few drinks, Shandy, I and a few others would go off for a curry supper.

In my early games for Lansdown, Les Angell was the opening bat. He had previously been captain for a number of years. Season after season he topped the batting averages. He had played for Somerset in the Harold Gimblett days. I admired his technique and the watchfulness with which he played the new ball on a difficult pitch. He was never in a hurry like me.

Now Leslie, a quiet, likeable cricketer who knew the game inside out, had been given the job by Somerset to keep an eye on me. The county thought his opinion of me, at close quarters, would be useful. In almost my first senior match for Lansdown, against Clifton, the strong Bristol club, I found myself in a stand with Leslie. He opened and got 61. I went in at No. 3 and was 89 not out when we declared at tea. And Leslie nodded approvingly when I came in.

I still fancied myself as a bowler. I seemed to reinforce the point by opening, in my first game, with a wicket maiden. Then a fortnight later against a Wiltshire side, Corsham, I opened the bowling, sent down seven maidens and finished with 0–7 in eleven overs. Shandy, coming on in my place at first change, took six wickets. We won that day and Shandy slapped me on the back for my bowling. He wasn't so happy about my batting. I hit three fours almost as soon as I got to the wicket and was then caught off a lazy shot.

I made a quick half century against local rivals Bath whom we beat by two wickets. That, I gathered, was on a par with winning the Test series.

Trowbridge, also from Wiltshire, were a strong, capable side who apparently didn't take a great liking to me. I'm assured it wasn't on a personal basis. I began by bowling 14 overs at them and then hit a century in 76 minutes. And when we played them again in the August I made 146 not out against them. Seven of my last scoring strokes were sixes.

That was on the Lansdown ground and the poor Trowbridge bowlers got some stick from our partisan crowd.

Gerry Goodman, who for years had covered Lansdown's matches for Bath's evening paper, was more buoyant than ever.

I remember he used to do the farming notes, too. His happiest journalistic days, I'm told, were sitting in the sun at the Lansdown ground, pint in hand, watching me put the ball into the neighbours' gardens. After the second game with Trowbridge he wrote a story for his newspaper saying that Trowbridge thought 'it was unfair for Vivian Richards to be playing in local club cricket'. I don't know where Gerry picked up that—but it made a nice, flattering headline.

Against Frome, the Somerset club side, I was out first ball at No. 3 to a young chap who was about the tallest and thinnest I'd ever played against. He had a rather strange action and I tried to belt the first ball he hurled at me. I hit it with all the power I could muster and imagined that was a straight-driven four without any trouble at all. But this beanpole of a bowler somehow held on to the ball for a wonderful catch.

He didn't get his hat-trick but he deserved to. A few years later he said to me, 'I had to catch it, Vivian—it would have gone right through my stomach.'

His name was Colin Dredge, then the opening bowler and No. 3 bat for Frome. Later he was to become my teammate with Somerset. I was to admire his accuracy and wholehearted approach to the game. An unassuming young cricketer, his impressive entry to county cricket and his contribution to the successes of the 1978 season should not be forgotten.

As I looked at the scorebook that day, I thought there was something wrong with my eyes. Two Dredges opened the bowling, another one opened the batting. I was told there were seven brothers altogether.

We played sides like British Rail, Swindon and Optimists, for whom a good-natured local doctor, Richard Bernard, who had earlier played a few games for Gloucestershire I was told and was actually a relative of the great W. G. Grace, bowled me for 95. And then I was out for the same total, caught off the Imperial, Bristol, off-spinner John Allen, a brother of the former England bowler, David. That was quite a match for me. Earlier Imperial had declared at 178-4—and I took all four wickets, with one or two cheeky spinners thrown in.

Jim Abrahams is a Lansdown member who umpired the first

team after retiring as a player. He occasionally still turns out in mid-week games. In one of these we played the City of Bath Boys School. They had a master, bearded Pat Colbourne, a former Minor Counties player who also used to skipper Bath. 'He's the one you've got to watch', Jim told me. 'Keep an eye on his off-cutters.'

Jim and I, experience and youth I suppose, went to the wicket together to open the innings.

Afterwards, he said: 'You're a mystery to me. Here was I struggling all the time to ward the ball off my stumps from one of the most feared bowlers in local club cricket. And you kept hitting the ball like a bullet to square-leg, getting 50 in no time at all and then giving up your wicket when your job was done'.

I don't mention the incident boastfully. But I think it makes the point that too many cricketers—and that includes Test players—allow themselves to be beaten by an opponent's reputation. No player on the other side must ever be feared whether he's appearing for Australia or the City of Bath Boys School.

It was a good season for Lansdown. I finished top of the batting averages. What pleased us most of all was winning the Somerset Supporters' knock-out final at the County Ground. It was a 20-over game and this appealed to me. The opponents, Morlands, a Glastonbury side, held back their experienced bowler, Bryan Lobb the former county player, till the end. Reputations, as I've said, didn't mean anything to me. I hit his first three balls for 4, 6 and 6. I don't know if he also put in a kind word for me. My aggression that day apparently did me no harm at all. Somerset, as everyone was beginning to tell me, liked the bold stroke makers. And that's what I had to be rather than just a slogger.

Roy Kerslake, who had been captain of Somerset before becoming the cricket chairman, was by now getting regular bulletins on my progress. While I cut the grass and couldn't wait for my weekend games, some members of the committee were hearing my name mentioned for almost the first time. Some others, I guess, were already sick to death of hearing it from Mr Creed. They probably didn't approve of reimbursing the air fare to this country. You couldn't blame them. 'Who the devil is this Viv Richards', they were openly asking.

I'd gone to the nets in Taunton where Tom Cartwright, then the coach, took his first real look at me. I'm not sure he was too impressed. I was told he thought I should go and get some experience in league cricket for the time being.

In an Under-25 match against Gloucestershire at Bristol, I made a century. Tom Cartwright was watching and I understand that was when the good reports went back to headquarters in Taunton. Roger Knight was captaining Gloucestershire that day and he was generous enough to clap me most of the way back to the pavilion.

The Nevil Road dressing rooms were buzzing after that. 'If Somerset don't take him, we should', was one inside comment that got back to me.

But I was still in limbo, centuries or not. I continued thankfully taking my pound-a-day pocket money. When I asked the county vice-chairman whether he thought I was going to be taken on by Somerset, he said: 'Of course, you are'. But he didn't seem to say it with too much conviction.

One reason was their interest about this time in the Australian Graeme Watson. They were looking for another overseas player and Watson, who had already played League cricket in this country and had represented his country, was certainly better known than this shy, bat-flashing Vivian Richards from an island in the West Indies that the English didn't associate with cricket.

Social life was at least better now in Bath. I liked the character of the little country pubs around Bath. The Kings Head at Weston village was one favourite. So was the Pack Horse at South Stoke, where I was taught to play shove ha'penny and tried in vain to beat Alan Bees.

I'd sit for hours in Grant's nightclub where apparently I was the first black member. The music was cool. There were shaded lights and pretty girls with cute West Country accents. The atmosphere excited me. I used to go there regularly with other members of the cricket club. I assured them it was my scene. It was steamy and rhythmic; my shoulders swayed. It was more like home.

Bath had several good jazz clubs, some of them in the local pubs. I visited most of them, content to listen most of the time. In an odd way I preferred not to talk about cricket in the evenings. Maybe I felt I would never make it in England and that it was all a waste of time.

I didn't drive a car in those days—and certainly couldn't have afforded one. I relied on my cricketing friends for lifts to matches and trips out to the village pubs or jazz clubs. One evening Alan Bees took me to a hall near Dursley in Gloucestershire to hear some jazz. On the way home we both decided we were hungry. There was always a hot-dog stand in Bath's London Road until about 1 a.m. My driver put his foot down.

They used to say I never missed a trick, that I had eyes in the back of my head. It could be useful when Saturday night cricketers were heading for home in the car, thinking about the winning hit rather than the looming breathalyser. My driver wasn't over the top with his drinking on the way back from Dursley but he was exceeding the speed limit in a built-up area.

Very calmly I turned to him and said: 'There's a police car following us'.

At that moment we came to traffic lights and there was another vehicle between us and the patrol car. As the lights changed we surged away, doubling back and for the next ten minutes sped around the side roads alongside Lansdown Road. The police car chased us at first but gradually we lost it.

I sighed and turned to my driver. 'Christ, Alan, it's just like the Mafia!'

That was one of my few brushes, indirect as it was, with the law. If that's what it's like, I'll stick to nicking mangoes back in Antigua.

But even my hairy car dash around the back streets of Bath, chased by a police car, wasn't as frightening, on reflection, as the night when several young St John's schoolboys were up a tree helping ourselves to sapodillas. We were filling our arms and felt satisfied with the haul. Then suddenly the limb of the tree broke and crashed on to the roof of the owner's house.

Imagine it happening in the still of the night. We tumbled out of the tree and the sapodillas rolled everywhere. In seconds all the lights in the house were switched on and the owner appeared at the window, shot-gun in hand. He wasn't particular whom he hit. He had been woken and was very angry. Muttering old Antiguan oaths and invoking the Humbies to catch us, he fired twice into the tree. Trembling and guilt-ridden, we scarpered. The four of us readily left our stolen fruit on the ground.

If there is a road traffic policeman back in Bath who remembers that mad car chase back in 1973, I plead guilty on behalf of my driver. I spotted you first and must take my share of the blame. For the record I don't approve of speeding round in the early hours of the morning. I don't like hurrying anyway—it isn't my style. I'm a stroller by nature. When I walk a single rather than run it, that's me. When I do the slow-march back to the pavilion, that's me.

In the same way I sauntered round the streets in Bath. I was always well-groomed, even though my modest earnings as assistant groundsman didn't go far. There were the economies I could make. Good friends, male and female, were often inviting me home for a meal. If I went out to eat, apart from my Saturday night curry with Shandy, I was happy with a snack. The first meal I bought out in Bath was at the Bell Inn, in Walcot Street. I took my time choosing from the simple menu—and then came up with mushrooms on toast. I think it cost 20p. My appetite isn't big for someone who is young, healthy and active. I think I surprised some of my cricket friends at Lansdown when they first discovered I had a weakness for beetroot—raw. They are as sweet and juicy as any apple.

After the early accommodation difficulties, I stayed briefly with the Jenkins twins, Peter and David, friends of mine who played for Lansdown, and I also found homely and happy digs with Mrs Joan Oliver and her family. I'd sit for hours at night, bare-footed in front of the fire, watching the television.

They had an elderly aunt who arrived to stay with them. She was told that they had a lodger, nothing more. When she came to go up the stairs, she had her first sight of me on the landing. I don't know if I was the first black man she had encountered close-up. In any case, I apparently scared the living daylights out of her.

59

The Olivers made me very welcome. They claimed they always had a job getting me up in the morning and making sure I got to the matches on time. I was never conscious of it being a bit of a rush. I used to catch the No. 204 bus, I remember, with young Martin Oliver. We'd get off at one point because I couldn't resist buying doughnuts and cream cakes. Then we'd pick up the bus again to take us to near the Lansdown ground.

At times I used to take Martin out on the back lawn for some cricket practice. But he and his family had the impression that I preferred football to cricket in those days. I must admit my enthusiasm for cricket was at times a bit on the wane. It was all that damned cold weather. Who wants to play cricket in the cold? Was it any wonder that I shivered all day—and then sat at night in front of the fire?

The last time I heard from Mrs Oliver, she was apologetic. I couldn't understand why.

'You know the bedroom wall that you kindly autographed for us, Vivian?'

I didn't know what was coming.

'Oh dear, I've gone and papered over it. And now you are famous!'

I've mentioned my footballing days back in Antigua. My father and brothers were good enough to play for the island. So was I, as a defender with a strong tackle and good sense of positional play.

During my season at Lansdown I was invited to go along for a trial with Bath City F.C., the Southern League Club. There are various versions of how I was asked along. Anyway the chairman of Bath City at that time was Gilbert Walshaw. It's said he was excitedly told one day by one of the Lansdown boys: 'We've got a cricketer with us who's good enough to play for Somerset. He's a great prospect. But he reckons he's better at soccer.'

They anxiously awaited an assessment of my footballing talents.

And then, rather cruelly, it arrived from Bath City. 'Bloody awful!' was the so-called verdict.

I didn't believe it! You should have seen me captaining the Grammar School. . . .

But I at least knew I had to concentrate and get those fleeting ideas of a Wembley appearance out of my system. The trouble was I'd gone to watch Arsenal and Leeds United during those impressionable days when I was in London to attend Alf Gover's school. And I'd romanced a bit ever since.

Before the end of the season I was invited to play in a testimonial match for Mervyn Kitchen, the popular Somerset professional. It was in a village near Bristol, not far from Mervyn's home. David Allen was playing, I remember. He had toured the West Indies as a young off-spinner and it was quite a thrill to see him back enjoying himself in village cricket.

I was sent in first with a tall, blond, broad-shouldered chap, carrying just a little bit of extra weight round the middle. We got on well and I could see he was a player of experience. I liked the way he went for his shots. He had my attitude to the game. Later I discovered he was David Green, the former Lancashire and Gloucestershire opening bat.

I made some quick, confident runs that day. Mervyn Kitchen was pleased. The village crowd, geographically more Gloucestershire than Somerset, enjoyed themselves. And David Green and David Allen, whose opinions I valued, both said some very encouraging things.

Somerset dithered, and I wondered whether my English cricket experience would be limited to sixes against Trowbridge, mower blisters on my hands and a few sneaky drinks from the club bar.

But Graeme Watson was forgotten—and recommendations from people like Les Angell helped.

'They're taking you, Vivian. Somerset are offering you a two-year contract.'

Now, I was told, it was up to me. That night I was given an extra celebration drink.

The terms were all I could reasonably expect. They were the same as any uncapped player with Somerset. But with bonuses on top I worked out that I could pocket something like £2,000.

Most Packer players are reckoned to be mercenaries and I'll have something to say about that later. At the time Mr Creed told me Somerset were going to take me on their staff, I couldn't have cared a fig what I was being paid.

I still didn't know what it was all about. It wasn't a question of being bought cheaply—of playing for peanuts as it seems, looking back now.

I had made it. I was about to join my old Barbadian 'star' Hallam Moseley in first-class cricket.

That September I flew home to Coolidge Airport in a new snazzy shirt, feeling like a champion. Miriam and all my friends were waiting. My parents were beaming.

'You've done it then, Vivi', said my father.

'Not yet', I said. 'I'm joining Somerset—now I've got to get some big scores for them.'

It still didn't enter my head that I might one day play for the West Indies. I looked out of the window of my home in Drake Street at the yard where Mervyn and I had played with our home-made bat. Our private Test Matches, carrying the marvellous fantasies of youth, were as taut and exciting as Kingston, Sydney or Lord's.

My father called me to one side. He hadn't approved of my indecision and the hanging-around aimlessly back in Antigua. He didn't really want me flying off to somewhere called Oldham or even somewhere less well-known called Lansdown when he argued it was about time I got down to studies and tried to earn some honest money for myself.

'The studies in New York are still there if you want to take them up. But cricket for Somerset may be an even better way of using your talents', he said.

I nodded. I don't often show my emotions unless, as happened in 1976, I managed to run-out three opponents for my country; or when Somerset beat Essex off the final ball in the Gillette Cup.

But my father could see how excited I was that evening back in Drake Street.

With Somerset

I arrived at Taunton for the pre-season nets in 1974 and was told
by the secretary of that time, Mr Jimmy James, a man with a
brisk no-nonsense manner who had worked as a civil servant in
Central and East Africa, that accommodation had been arranged
for me.

Based on my experiences in Bath, I privately hoped this time
for a nice, homely landlady who would make sure I had a hot
meal each day.

'We're putting you into the club flat alongside the ground
here. You'll like that.'

There shouldn't be any problems about over-sleeping, I
thought to myself.

The secretary went on 'You'll be sharing the flat with two
other Somerset lads. Dennis Breakwell and Ian Botham'.

I didn't know any of the Somerset professionals well apart
from Hallam Moseley. In fact, I'd expected to be in the same
digs as him. That would have stopped any hint of home-
sickness.

During my summer at Lansdown I had travelled to Taunton
on the train for my coaching under Tom Cartwright. I liked the
county ground. It was small and friendly, just right for sixes
when the bowler pitched short. Whenever I went to a cricket
ground I liked to look round the boundary. Especially in the
direction of mid-wicket and extra cover.

The secretary's office was a small, green wooden building
alongside the car park. It was crammed with files, stacks of old
photographs, faded testimonial brochures and all the usual office
equipment. Mr James was partitioned off at one end. Conditions

seemed cramped and there was little elbow room for the staff. The dressing-rooms were a let-down. They were an improvement on some of the ropey ones I'd known. But they were certainly more dungeon-like than some in good-class club cricket. Everywhere seemed so dark and it was even worse for the visitors as I discovered later when I returned as a member of the West Indies side playing against Somerset. The Taunton dressing-rooms, were, I assure you, not the last word in comfort. Players used to moan about the facilities and they had the backing of the club. In 1978 the president Colin Atkinson launched his appeal to improve things.

Tony Lewis tells a nice story, suitably embellished, from his Glamorgan days. He claims that one member of the team, who came from a mining family, argued that a collier would normally have sent down a fireman with a canary into a place like the visitors' room at Taunton to test for gas. But the canary, he reckons, would have snuffed it halfway down the stairs. 'Waiting down there with the pads on', says Tony, tongue-in-cheek, 'was like being trapped underground, and we used to joke that only our coal-mining heritage got us through the three days'.

I had once been driven down to Taunton from Bath to watch a Gillette Cup match against Leicestershire the previous year. Brian Close, I remember, was out immediately before lunch. I sat in the members' enclosure for almost the whole of the game. They say I got very excited. The fact is, I'm not a good spectator. I wanted to be out there on the pitch.

After the game I was introduced to most of the players. I doubt if any of them had taken in my name. I was just another trialist passing through. Professional cricketers are, with good reason, often on the defensive. Their main aim must be to get their contract renewed; any newcomer means one job less for the others on the playing staff.

Now I was back—as one of them. I tried on my kit self-consciously and didn't do much talking. Some of the other young professionals, I noticed, were also very quiet. Everything was new to me—the cricket language, the training routine, the chat about expenses, the speculation about who would be in the team for the first game.

Somerset's opening fixture was against Glamorgan at Swansea in the Benson and Hedges competition. I hoped I'd be included. But I was still unproven and they might decide to give me my chance later. The team was announced—and I was in. I wanted to phone home and tell them. Not on an uncapped player's pay, I told myself. The date still sticks happily in my memory: April 27.

I didn't even know where Swansea was. The car journey up the motorway and over the Severn Bridge seemed to go on for ever. As usual I didn't have much to say. I was worrying whether I had all my kit, a clean shirt, my toothbrush and my deodorant . . . I was the new boy and feeling out of place. Hallam, cheerful as ever, was assuring me we could beat Glamorgan.

We did beat them. Brian Close sent me in at No. 4 and I helped to steer Somerset home by six wickets with 81 not out. Glamorgan, I remember, had made 194–5 in their 55 overs. Between innings I heard all those strange Welsh voices. They thought they had enough on the board. But Brian Close put us on course with 31, 'Dasher' Denning followed on with 40—and I stayed till the end. I was nervous when I first walked to the wicket. And I was nearly as bad when they handed me the gold award. If this was county cricket, I thought to myself in the bar later, I was going to enjoy myself.

I was feeling elated as I came off the field. I knew I had passed my test. The confidence, which seldom deserts me once I am at the wicket, grew all the time as my cover drives sped on a fast outfield to the boundary. I resisted the temptation to loft the shots to mid-wicket. I didn't try to put the ball into the Mumbles at Swansea.

There was a surprise waiting for me as I came in. I looked up and suddenly saw all the Somerset team at the bottom of the pavilion steps, lining the route for me and applauding. They slapped me on the back. 'You'll do for me', Brian Close said.

Then I spotted Len Creed. He was crying. He put his arm round me. 'Thanks, Vivian. I knew I was right to bring you back.'

A hard-bitten bookmaker crying? He was, as I was to find

out, as soft and sentimental as the cussing Brian Close.

I can't begin to say what applause from my fellow professionals meant to me. I'd like to think it was spontaneous but that isn't quite true. I was told later that the players were intently watching the final strokes from the first floor vantage point when the skipper turned to them and said: 'Come on, you buggers. Down those stairs. I want you to clap young Vivian off the field.'

The adjudicator that day was Charlie Barnett, a former Gloucestershire opening batsman, who, I'm told, liked to get on with it. Perhaps he approved of my attempt to make strokes all the time.

Mr Creed said to him afterwards, 'I was terrified, Charlie. Frightened to bloody death that Vivian would fail.'

The generous reply was, 'He's going to be one of the world's greats'.

And the county skipper added, 'This, Len, is the best thing you've ever done for Somerset cricket.'

There was no danger of my taking such praise too seriously. It washed off me. I'd got a few centuries for Lansdown the previous season . . . and been out first ball to Colin Dredge. It was still a great start for my morale but I knew there would be harder matches on more difficult wickets. The encouraging thing was that I'd proved to my more experienced and, I expect, sceptical teammates that I could play a bit.

Back in Taunton some of the fans started making a fuss of me. They would point me out as I went down the street at night to buy the fish-and-chips. The rumours mounted. 'He turned down an academic career to come to Somerset, you know. Had a college lined up in New York.'

Sadly I was never quite as bright as that academically. Newspaper reports have suggested that I had 5 A-levels. In truth, I didn't get one. And as for college life in New York, it would have probably been work by day, and night school studies afterwards.

I had a few days lodging at that cricket-mad Taunton pub the Crown and Sceptre and then moved in with Dennis and Ian. My flat-mates were a lively pair. I shared a room with Dennis who was temporarily sampling bachelor life again after a broken marriage. 'Both', not yet 20 and fresh from the Lord's staff, was full of life. He was supremely self-confident even then. I envied him the assurance he seemed to bring to everything he did on or off the field. I knew it was a vital attribute of the successful professional sportsman. We had, the three of us, differing personalities. But we did a lot of things together and had plenty of fun, some of it unplanned.

I have never been a big drinker, although I acquired a modest taste for Guinness in Bath. There is some steady drinking done by county cricketers in the course of a season.

Ian came from the South Somerset town of Yeovil. His parents continued to live there and once or twice he took me down to meet them. Then he would lead me off to some of the pubs and haunts he knew. We'd meet up with his old school pals.

With an outward-going guy like Ian, it was hard not to paint the town red. We had a few, I remember, at a club in the town and a bloke there ordered the pair of us out. To this day I don't really know why. We weren't causing a disturbance.

Ian wasn't yet an established member of the Somerset side but he had no doubts about his own ability to make it. I admired the way he went for his shots and had a lovely follow-through. Even then, as a bowler, he was making the ball swing a lot. Brian Close would jump on any of the young pros if they seemed to be getting over-ambitious. He would put them in their place with a cutting remark. Some of them felt he was less than fair to them. In fact, they have blossomed since his departure. Dennis Breakwell, although not exactly one of the youngest professionals, is perhaps an example of this. He didn't get too much scope, it could be argued, under Brian.

We had basic cooking facilities in our club flat. Occasionally we tried our luck with a bit of steak or got someone's girl friend in to grill it for us. I fancied myself at frying eggs! We didn't go short. We were among the best customers at the local fish-and-chip shop. I'd never had them back in Antigua and I was soon an addict in Taunton.

The three of us kept late hours. Dennis was the worst of the three, although he didn't seem to need much sleep. He was usually last in at night—and first up in the morning, whistling brightly to himself.

Three unattached bachelors might have been expected to cause the occasional disturbance. Not at all. We kept the flat tidy—at least one of the girl friends did—and we welcomed the convenience of being so near the ground. Strangely, we hardly ever talked cricket.

Irregular sleep, I hate to admit, was gradually catching up on me, however. It was all very well for Dennis. He bounced in, humming to himself, and was snoring almost as soon as he hit the pillow. I was always a light sleeper. 'You're looking tired, Viv', my friends began to say.

Tactfully I pulled out from the shared flat for the next season I was back. I remained the best of friends with Dennis and Ian. But I decided I had to settle down for a while. I went to stay with Terry and Trissie Smith, along with Hallam. This was a happy relaxed arrangement. It was more like home and I started catching up on my sleep. I had someone looking after the laundry again. I could stay in and watch the television if I wished. I knew every Kojak and Starsky-and-Hutch story-line backwards.

But watching television every night isn't, I'm beginning to realise, really my scene. I get restless. Taunton is a fairly quiet market town and you have to make your own social life. I have always done rather well in that direction. Terry and Trissie Smith gave me the steadying influence I needed but it wasn't fair for me to remain there for ever. Late-night phone calls for me were always coming. And as I stayed out later again, life at 19, French Way seemed a bit restricting. In more recent years I have had a basement flat at the home of Somerset secretary Roy Stevens, the man who took over from Jimmy James. I have my own key—and my own life. This gives me the independence I need. I don't upset anyone with 2 a.m. phone calls. I can bring friends home without worrying about whether I'm keeping someone awake. I sit for hours listening to my stereo. This is when the Detroit Spinners, Gladys Knight and the Pips or Teddy Pendergrass sound best of all. For half the year I'm living out of a suitcase, staying in hotels with their bustle and passing-through traffic, and not much chance to play my albums. My flat in Taunton isn't perhaps the last word in luxury. But it is private. I keep it tidy because I'm a tidy guy. If there are more LPs and shirts than anything else it's because they reflect two of my passions.

I didn't have as many, of course, when I first moved in with Dennis and Ian. There wouldn't have been any room for them, anyway.

What did I make of all my new teammates? I was still too shy—or perhaps tactful—to open my mouth with any strong personal feelings. The Somerset boys, wary at first, had seen me giving the ball a good licking against Glamorgan. And I think I was accepted from that moment.

Opinions about Brian Close vary so much. His blunt manner brings him a few enemies. He isn't always too fussy about what he says. Not everyone inside the Somerset dressing room might have named him as their No. 1 idol. I used to eavesdrop on the occasional remarks, not always completely complimentary, when they were flying around out of his earshot.

I'm not suggesting that the Somerset dressing room was an unhappy one. When you get a crowd of professional sportsmen living in and out of each others' pockets all through the season, fearing in some cases for their next contract and always their next run of bad luck at the wicket, clashes of personality are bound to go on.

It has been said that Brian Close gave a rough ride to some of the younger pros. I honestly didn't see too much evidence of this. He blasted any players, not just the young ones, when they had a snooze in the field. If it was done publicly, I expect they resented it.

The skipper's name had a magical ring to it a long time before I came to Somerset. Back in Antigua as a small boy I used to hear it mentioned on the radio during the cricket commentaries. I listened to the way he stuck out his chest to Wes Hall and Charlie Griffiths. He sounded one hell of a cricketer to me. Those two bowlers were really dangerous and here was someone who wasn't frightened of them. Close was respected in the West Indies. We like gutsy players.

So what kind of a bloke was he? I wanted to find out. After all they reckoned he was the best captain in England—and now he was going to be my skipper.

It didn't take me long to be on the receiving end. He pulled me to one side and said, 'With all that bloody talent, why don't you graft a bit more?'

That was telling me. No-one had summed me up so quickly and scathingly before. But he did it fairly—and with a faint smile on his face.

Nice of the skipper to talk of my talent. He was being serious though about the way I played the game. My style didn't have much to do with Yorkshire or the way he'd been brought up to make things hard for the other side. I was still, I suppose, in attitude, really a week-end cricketer entertaining my mates in St John's.

After his rollicking I went back to my shared flat and thought about what he'd said. Yes, I was inclined to be a lazy type on the field. I was apt to dream and lose myself during the game. And Brian Close was telling me, 'Stop messing about. Change your attitude, Vivian. It isn't enough to have a natural talent.' I think I got the message.

He took to me, not just because I helped to put a few win bonuses our way. As he drank his whisky after a game he had a habit of wondering aloud why I had clipped that simple catch to short mid-wicket. 'It was no sense, lad—you were there for the day.'

I liked the way he crouched at short square-leg. He feared nothing, I told myself. 'That bugger's made of iron' other players used to whisper, half-admiringly. Later, when he pulled off his shirt, we sometimes saw the bruises. He pretended they didn't exist but probably was glad we noticed them.

Fear certainly meant nothing to him, either, when he was driving his car. All through his cricket career I understand players reckoned their number was up when they found they were travelling in his car.

I used to travel with Brian quite a lot for away matches. I'm not exactly the slowest thing on four wheels, although I don't claim to be quite in Ian Botham's class for speed. Closey was still the master. Coming back from the Scarborough Festival once with him I was holding on grimly to the arm-rest, wishing that I'd remembered to put on my seat belt. The Close foot was hard down and he was strangely silent. I looked at him out of the corner of my eye and suddenly realised that he was asleep. Driving fast through the night with a driver who has his eyes closed is a nasty feeling. I shouted, 'Skip!'

He jumped up in his seat, instinctively concentrated on the road ahead and then gave me a long, withering look.

'It's all right, lad.'

Brian Close's last season or two with Somerset didn't always see him at his best. He felt that one or two of the Somerset committee members were getting on his back. They said he was staying away from the county too much and was chasing one or two of the young pros unreasonably. He never had too much time for committees—and in confidential moments he'd tell me what he thought of county cricket officials who'd never played the game.

In my opinion he remained a good captain until he left Somerset. He was always in the game and gave nothing away. As a player he was still useful and he took some of the best catches I've ever seen.

Most of the team used to fall asleep at times during the game. I expect Brian Rose, later to become Close's successor, would admit that he used occasionally to dream on the field. The old, wily skipper detected our dreaming. Some, frankly, didn't like too much the way he let them know.

But he could also be soft-hearted and generous with his racing tips. I don't gamble much myself but I'm not sure the information he received about the ones that couldn't lose was too reliable. I wonder how consistently 'Budgie' Burgess and Merv Kitchen followed the skipper's tips. Studying form and making for the nearest phone in the press box at the tea interval were sights of the skipper that always amused me.

I like being surrounded by young players in the team. They are still learning and generally eager for advice. Peter Roebuck is the one I tip for an England place. He looks so deadly serious in his glasses and I can imagine him as a lawyer. That is what he'll probably be after giving up his cricket. When he came down first from Cambridge he was always walking round the boundary between innings with his law books under his arms.

It's true I've taken a fatherly interest in Peter even though I'm only a few years older. Nearly every time I've seen him play I've been impressed. They say he hasn't got so many shots. Well, I've seen cricketers with fewer shots than him play for England. It's temperament that also counts—and Peter seems to have no worries there. He's a great thinker about the game. All the time he's at the wicket he's mentally ticking over, analysing every stroke and checking on every change in the field.

I've seen the young players of Somerset grow—in confidence, I mean. Colin Dredge, cheeky enough to get me first ball when I came to England first, pegs usefully off that slightly ungainly delivery of his. Keith Jennings came as an in-swinger; now he's cutting the ball back the other way and is reminding me a bit of Tom Cartwright.

And then there is 'Both'. His self-confidence is at times misunderstood. I know him as an old flat mate and a friend. I knew he would play for England—and I suspect he did, too. But his entry to Test cricket was, even so, far more spectacular than he could have dreamt. There are selfish players in the professional game and we could all name them.

Ian Botham is very much a team man. He is willing to have a slog at any time if that is what his skipper wants from him. He rides his luck—and he deserves to. With so many years of cricket ahead of him as an all-rounder, he looks like having a page or two all to himself in Wisden.

There are quite a few stories told about Hallam Moseley, all with affection. In his first season with Somerset he took part in a benefit match on a village ground and had to run and retrieve the ball from a clump of stinging nettles. He dived straight in with no thought for his hands, not knowing what nettles are. Cricketers have a cruel sense of humour and they doubled-up as an alarmed Hallam started leaping for safety—without the ball. He's also inclined to be absent-minded and he once took the field as a No. 11 at The Oval with gloves and box . . . but no pads. He'd forgotten them. A gentle reminder and he rushed back to strap them on. He's a great sleeper—and I'm not talking now about during a game. That bloke Moseley could sleep on a clothes-line, I'm telling you. I've known him fall asleep in the middle of a conversation.

I don't believe in being quite as casual as Hallam at The Oval but there's no point, I reckon, in getting all prepared and keyed-up ages before it's my turn to bat. I don't often watch the play. I thumb through the Sun or the Telegraph—my range is pretty wide as you'll see—or I nod off. When they're out or it's raining, players are apt to play cards. Not me; I wander away to the treatment room for a kip. Who needs early nights when there's a comfortable table in the treatment room?

The lads know where I am and call me for tea.

During my first season, while I was living in the club flat, I decided to walk across the car park to my bed as soon as I was out. There was still most of the innings left as I flopped out on my sheets and was asleep almost at once. Much later I woke with a start, panicked, ran back to the dressing-rooms. Our last batsmen were just coming off the field. The timing couldn't have been better.

But I'm not sure what Tom Cartwright thought when I failed to turn up for net practice one morning. It was dark and overcast and I reckoned it was about 5 o'clock in the morning. I grunted and went back to sleep. Almost immediately there was a phone call. The secretary Jimmy James was on the line. Rather frostily he said, 'Tom is enquiring about you'.

I took another look out. Yes, it was pretty dark. But the players were all out there at net practice. I dressed quickly and mumbled my apologies. In fact, I didn't like early mornings at Taunton any more than I did at Bath.

Early-season practice has never been my favourite pursuit. I can pound round the county ground—and have often done it just to show the other lads that a late night doesn't kill me off for the morning. My Test commitments meant that more than once I missed the training sessions at Taunton. Frankly it didn't fill me with regret.

A good relationship with the coach is important. I get on quite well with Peter Robinson. His sense of humour appeals to me.

Early in the 1978 season the runs weren't coming as regularly as they should have.

'Have a look, Peter, and tell me where I'm going wrong', I said.

We had a long, thoughtful spell together. I wasn't getting to the pitch of the ball. I was going only halfway and my feet were all wrong. We solved my little problem together.

That 1974 season wasn't at all a bad one for Somerset. Nor, I suppose, for me. The county finished fifth in the championship table, they got to the semi-final of the Benson and Hedges and the Gillette, and only that lousy British weather made sure they didn't pick up the John Player trophy.

Father-figure Len Creed, soon to become chairman of the county, dug me in the ribs and said, 'You've picked the right side, Vivian. You did well not to go Lancashire!'

So many things that happened that summer made an impression on me. Closey told everyone he didn't like the Sunday game but I noticed he hit a record number of sixes, and managed a couple of centuries in the 40 overs. He also had his first 'pair' and we sympathised with him. It was the season that Ian Botham got his chance because Tom Cartwright was injured—and when a schoolmaster, Bob Clapp, surprised everyone, including himself, by taking a record number of wickets in the John Player competition. That likeable student with his head nearly always in a book when he wasn't on the field, Peter Roebuck, also came in for two or three matches.

We shouldn't have done so well that season. Mervyn Kitchen wasn't fit all the time. But Derek Taylor was tried as an opening bat. In a matter of weeks he'd scored 179 and set up a new fourth-wicket record with Brian Close (96). Not bad for someone who wasn't really rated and was said to have no scoring shots.

Cricket was just beautiful for me after that opening game at Swansea when I got into the money for the first time with the gold award. Half the cash goes into the players' pool, of course. But I was feeling rich—and in good nick at the same time. The Glamorgan bowlers hadn't looked too difficult that day and if that was county cricket, I told myself, I could get by.

I followed up with 71 in the next Benson and Hedges match on an overcast day when I thought it was the middle of winter. Peter Denning pipped me for the award with a knock of 87. I was soon to learn why they called him 'Dasher'. He streaked up and down that wicket as though he was training on red meat. Come to think of it he probably was. His father is a local butcher!

The Taunton wicket was pretty much to my liking. Apart from the first few overs in the morning you could trust it.

I don't know what to say about the one at Torquay where we went for the next match, against Minor Counties (South). The place was full of holiday-makers in their deckchairs. It was only a few yards from the seafront and I thought it was a pretty enough ground. But one with a difficult wicket. We did win in the end by six wickets and I made a half-century with a succession of shots, often uncertain, that weren't even in the Antigua Grammar School class all the time. Just as well Minor Counties made only 118. We lost Kitchen (6), Close (0), and Denning (9) in no time at all.

By now the lads were fancying their chances in the one-day competitions. I was taking them as they came. I can't say I played any differently whether the game went on for one or three days. At times someone would say: 'Get your nut down, Viv'. And I tried.

We went back to Taunton for the quarter finals against Hampshire. That was a special match for me. Andy Roberts on one side and me on the other. Two boys who'd made it together from Antigua and who played side by side for Rising Sun were now competing against each other. It seemed strange to the pair of us. We chatted before the game, friendly as ever.

'I'll get you today, Viv', were his parting words. In fact, I had a poor match, although fortunately 'Both' didn't. He was 18 and played as though he'd been around for years. He went in at No. 9, got hit in the mouth by Andy, spat the blood out and made 45 not out. Hallam Moseley, who in those days prided himself on his flailing bat at No. 10, scored 24. We won by one wicket.

The semi-final was at Leicester and we were done by 140 runs. Closey, I remember, had a moan about the pitch. I didn't blame him. It was bare in places and turned into a nasty turner when play went into a second day. Ray Illingworth was doing all sorts of things with the ball.

Leicestershire didn't reckon we had much grounds for our protest. They pointed out that they'd still made 270–8. I suppose that is a pretty strong argument. I was top scorer for Somerset with 42 but already I was finding that there could be some very funny wickets in England and if I didn't keep playing forward I'd be in trouble.

All county cricketers acquire impressions of other clubs over the years—the friendlier ones, the complainers, those that never stop shouting for LBW, those that can't wait to have a drink with you afterwards.

I've got nothing specifically against the Leicestershire players but it pleases me to do well against them. They have a good professional team but from my experience the bowlers moan like hell.

From the time I played my first match on a hard, dusty track at home, I've hated moaners. Ask any county cricketer who are the moaning bowlers in England and he'll come up with the same two or three names.

We all play and miss sometimes. But the one thing I can't stand is the comment that follows in the case of one or two bowlers. 'You jammy bugger.'

My response is always the same. I've done it numerous times since I started playing for Somerset. I don't say anything—I just point at the scoreboard. It's my way of saying, 'I'm not doing so badly, you belly-acher.' If I can take advantage of that kind of bowler, I will. It's the only time in cricket that I harbour a grudge.

I also know English bowlers, well-known names, who fancy themselves as psychologists. They get the occasional ball past the bat and they stand with their hands on their hips, staring at me as if I'm the luckiest player on the field. I simply stare back at them. My eyes, I'm told, flash menacingly. As I get older—and wiser to the tricks of the professional sportsman—I become more and more convinced of one thing. The world isn't one-sided. Sometimes it's going to be that glowering bowler's day as he brings one back off the seam. But often it's going to be my day as well—and I'm going to take full advantage.

As far as my three-day experience was concerned in that first season, it had begun with a drawn match against the Indians at Taunton. It was my chance to study Tom Cartwright close up. He bowled beautifully in that match and it was a pity that his stay with Somerset wasn't happier in the end. I was rather glad I was away and out of the trouble when, after two seasons of recurring injuries, he fell out with the county and wouldn't play for them. The result was that he was suspended and then came the end of his contract.

By the end of May I was seemingly being played as an all-rounder—whatever a few of my teasing friends in Bath thought of my gentle seamers and off breaks. At Hove I bowled 22 overs and took two wickets. I don't know how that fine Somerset off-spinner Brian Langford viewed me as his successor. We had a joke or two about it.

There were too many draws for my liking. Against Northants at Taunton I chanced my arm in the second innings with 62 in 43 minutes. Five quick sixes and five fours seemed to please the Somerset farmers who used to come across the road from the market. But another draw. I got fed up shivering and running in from the showers. 'How do you guys ever manage to concentrate?' I asked.

We won at last against Kent. It was an important game for me because Colin Cowdrey was in the visitors' team. His kind remarks about me, recorded in a cricket magazine, had brought me to England.

I thought back to the match when apparently I made a bit of a mark with him. Kent had gone over to the West Indies and played against Antigua. I made 65 that day. It wasn't my own innings that excited me that afternoon on the St John's Recreation Ground; it was the fact that I was turning out against a captain of England. He, like Brian Close, was one of those cricket heroes whose name used to come over loud and clear on my radio as I listened to the commentary.

We had a very brief chat in Antigua and I remember he complimented me on my knock. And now we were having a few

Above left At Taunton with Len Creed.
Above right With the old skipper—Brian Close.
Below Three great bowlers! Myself, Joel 'Big Bird' Garner, Hallam Moseley.

pleasant words again, when he came to Taunton. I don't know what he thought of the West Indians as hosts on his Caribbean visit. We showed him little consideration as he walked to the Taunton wicket. Hallam got him for one in the first innings and eight in the second. Barbadians have quite a tough streak, of course!

A young bloke called Bob Woolmer, later to be a Packer colleague of mine, made his maiden century in that match against Somerset. He also got me out LBW—but not before I'd made 85.

That really was a fantastic match. It's still, to my mind, one of the best championship wins Somerset have had since I've been with them. They were 131–5 with 70 minutes left. That meant they had no chance. Most of the supporters had gone home, anyway. And then 'Budgie' Burgess and Brian Close flung their bat at everything to put on 93 in 38 minutes. Graham was dropped three times and Kent got more and more rattled. He hunched his big Somerset shoulders and took 23 off an over from Johnson. He scored 67 and moved faster between the wickets than I've ever seen him before or since. Closey, with a sense of drama, finished it all with a six. We were incredibly 274–6 and had won.

Then, for me, it was on to Bath where I wanted to do well in front of my old mates from Lansdown—and the steel band boys from Russell Street. It was a tricky pitch as it usually is. But I settled into a big stand with Mervyn Kitchen and finished with 107. It was my first century in the championship and the members got up to applaud me as I came in.

The atmosphere is completely different at Bath. I like the festival feeling and the beer-tent where, if we're lucky, the bar is still open after we've showered. And usually there's an invitation from the sponsor's tent. Some of the players say they prefer playing on one ground or the other. It doesn't bother me. They may not look alike but what strikes me all the time, the supporters are almost entirely the same. I spot the familiar red faces on the boundary whether we're playing at Bath, Weston, Taunton or Glastonbury.

That, though, was a happy visit to Bath for me in 1974. We

also stuffed Gloucestershire and lost to Pakistan by only five runs. My flat-mate, Ian Botham, opened the bowling and took a wicket with his first ball. We batted fourth and scored 314—and that couldn't have been bad.

By this time, 'Both' was fancying his chances. By mid-July he'd hit his maiden half-century against Middlesex. His strength was already obvious and I admired the way he clouted accurate medium-paced bowling for a couple of sixes and seven fours. He certainly did better than me. A young bowler, Martin Vernon, playing only his third championship match for Middlesex, got me both times. He had a terrific match, with 6–58 and 5–54, and that takes some doing at Taunton. I was surprised to discover he'd given up county cricket within a matter of three years. He left Middlesex for Gloucestershire and they decided not to retain him. It sums up the uncertainty of sport as a wage-earner.

No game as complicated as cricket can escape controversy. Sports writers love it although when, as in the case of racial politcs, they try to prise a comment out of me, I grin silently. In the course of the summer we had plenty to natter about as we showered and changed. If it wasn't Closey's strong language about the Leicester wicket, it was the way umpires Barrie Meyer and Alan Whitehead made things tough for Nottinghamshire at Trent Bridge in August. Notts were due to bat last and when we lost our tenth wicket there were three of the final twenty overs still remaining. They only needed 17 runs so they looked good for a win.

But then came a drizzle and the umpires decided there was only time for two overs. Derek Randall opened with Hassan and they failed by three runs. I felt sorry for them.

Mike Smedley, the Nottinghamshire skipper, was far from pleased. He complained bitterly. 'The weather was no worse than when Somerset were batting', he argued. And I think he had a point—although I never want to present the other side with the points.

There was still the Weston-super-Mare Festival to come. 'Watch the ball, lad', said Brian Close to me. 'It can be a bloody funny wicket.'

He didn't have to tell me anything about Weston. I imagined

it was the spongy strip where I'd had my first game for Lansdown. It wasn't, of course. But Clarence Park, when it's damp, doesn't love batsmen. And it was damp when Leicestershire came. So damp, in fact, that we lost our first four wickets for eight runs. Closey's advice to me hadn't been much use.

I can remember that he was magnificent in that match. He hit 59 in the first innings and 114 not out in the second. I didn't kip when he was in. I marvelled at the way he used his feet and would then suddenly go down on one knee to belt the ball to the mid-wicket boundary like only a left-hander can. He wasn't the most stylish player I'd ever seen—and certainly not always the most tactful one. But I'll never forget how he got his runs at Weston.

Nor, come to that, will I forget how he lashed into bowlers as experienced as Tony Brown and Roger Knight when he took 128 off Gloucestershire earlier in the summer in the Sunday League. He did it with a certain contempt as if to say: 'I don't like this nonsense you call one-day cricket but if I've got to play it, I'll show you!'

We thought we were good enough to win the trophy. It all depended on the last game at Leicester. We needed four points and the game was never finished because of the rain. We'd already lost to Kent in the semi-final of the Gillette Cup and we had ended the season with nothing. It was to be the unhappy pattern over the next few years.

Back I came to England for 1975, Somerset's centenary year. They were selling their special brochures and pushing their membership. All they needed was a pot to put on the shelf for the perfect ending. Again they didn't smell a title. My own memories of the season vary sharply. I got my first championship double-century against Yorkshire—and was out for a pair when we played Northamptonshire. I also smashed a door in anger at Harrogate. Perhaps I'd better tell you about it.

We went to Yorkshire at the end of June. As usual Brian Close wanted to do well against them. And he did, with a gutsy 91. I also wanted to do well as Closey had told me they appreciated good cricket up there. 'Well done, lad' he said as I came in at the end of the first innings. I'd made 217 not out and Somerset were

423–7. That meant I'd been steaming a bit.

My double century was apparently only the third scored against Yorkshire since the war. Another Somerset man from the West Indies, Peter Wight, and Basil D'Oliveira scored the others. That was rubbing it in. No wonder Yorkshire have those unrelenting views about overseas players . . . .

The wicket had been full of runs as Jackie Hampshire found when he scored a first innings century. Yorkshire had it made, like us, and scored 387–9 and 335–7. But they left us to chase 300 runs batting last and it wasn't on.

The trouble was we made a complete mess of it when all we had to do, as each succeeding batsman was told, was to 'get your nut down'. Apart from young Phil Slocombe and Derek Taylor, the highest score was Graham Burgess. He managed four. In the end we somehow hung on at 116–9.

I didn't see the end of that match. I was deep in the dressing room, seething at an incident which maybe I should have been able to cope with differently.

But the tension had been building up as we panicked and tried to save the game. We'd been ten foot high with our massive first innings total and here we were facing defeat. Recriminations were beginning to fly around. 'Enough of these airy-fairy bloody shots, for Christ's sake stay there!' The skipper was pretty angry.

I had an ankle injury and knew that I wouldn't be able to chase quick singles. But I saw no reason why I couldn't stay till the end for the draw that we needed so badly. My partner was Derek Taylor and we both realised what we had to do. Suddenly he pushed the ball and called for a sharp single. I had to go, limping slightly, and I was run out. Friendly as I am with the Somerset stumper, I still think he was wrong to call for that unnecessary run. I had no quibble with the umpire—I was out.

Often after I'm out I meander back to the dressing room. I take my time, lost in my thoughts and privately furious that I have given my wicket away. That day at Harrogate, more ponderous than ever because of my ankle injury, I started my slow-march back. I daresay the crowd could see how I was feeling. I was very, very annoyed.

The spectators felt I was taking too long. And one suddenly shouted, 'Hurry up, you black bastard'.

It was flash-point for me. I looked up and glared in the direction of the insult. Then I moved very quickly indeed towards that group of spectators. I held my bat up and shouted, 'Whoever said that can get up.'

No-one did. They never do. I accept that it was an ugly moment. I must have held that bat menacingly and my eyes blazed.

My anger didn't subside. I stomped to the dressing room and smashed the door with my bat. It was the only way I could release my emotions.

I heard nothing from Yorkshire about the incident. My teammates didn't pursue the subject until I'd cooled it. Looking back at this distance I must be completely honest and say I regret nothing that I did. I hope you will understand.

That isn't, obviously, one of the happy memories of 1975. Two innings against Gloucestershire are. In a fabulous Sunday game of cricket at Bristol, we scored 270–4 and Gloucestershire replied with 255, beaten in the last over. There were two centuries: I made 126 not out and Sadiq 131 for Gloucestershire. When it came to the championship at Taunton in mid-August there was no play on the third day because of rain. But I'd already licked a quick 128. One of the oddest things about the game was that the most successful of our seven bowlers, including the skipper himself, were Brian Rose (3–9) and Richards (2–10).

We also had a Sunday match against Leicestershire at Yeovil where I hoped there was no nightclub owner, with a long mean memory, lurking in the crowd. My luck didn't change—I was out for a duck.

The ridiculous thing about that match was that a Leicestershire official made a great fuss at the start about the so-called short boundaries. Yet the visitors won when Norman McVicker straight drove the last two balls of the evening for towering sixes. Will poor Allan Jones, the bowler, ever forget it?

I was missing from Somerset for the whole of 1976 because of Test match commitments but I was contracted to return the next summer. That was the season that the county beat the Australians for the first time and that giant Joel Garner, on his debut for Somerset, took a wicket in his first over. It was the season when Ian Botham was selected for England and I scored nearly 3,000 runs in the various competitions for Somerset. 'Both' and 'Rosey' went on to win a place in England's winter tour.

How far should a cricketer risk boring his readers by cataloguing his best scores? Or risk being called a big-head? I have never kept a scrapbook and once an innings is played, even my better ones, it is soon a vague sort of memory. I get no kick out of instant re-plays over a drink; I accept congratulations with thanks but what successes and feats I've achieved really mean little to me once the game is over. If I should happen to go into the record book for something or other, so what? There are hundreds of people on the earth with a talent far more worthy of permanent recognition.

For my playing record in this book I have had to go back to Wisden for the actual scores. And they include my three double centuries in that 1977 season. I was a bit ruthless when it came to the Gloucestershire bowlers. At Bristol, where the wicket was slow but of little help to the bowlers, I scored 241 not out, in front of fewer than 400 spectators and after four interruptions for rain. In the bar afterwards one of Gloucestershire supporters said, 'Vivian, some of those cover drives reminded me of Wally Hammond.'

It was great, on the one hand, to hear him say it—as the famous England and Gloucestershire stylist looked down on us from the wall. But it also embarrassed me. Hammond, I know, wouldn't have made as many mistakes as me.

A few of the sports writers were going crazy about this time and saying I reminded them of other great players. Someone said, 'He's got the grace of Worrell and the killer instincts of Weekes.' I'd like to think I picked up some of the best qualities of these two West Indian heroes. But comparisons like that are pointless and make me hope that no-one is reading them.

Wisden, that reliable aid to the memory, claims that my 204 against Sussex was one of the best knocks ever seen on the Hove ground. I know we beat the home county by an innings. And my score was also 204 when we beat Surrey at Weston-super-Mare. I do remember plenty about that match. My innings, in early August, took me to my 2,000 runs for the season. Peter Roebuck, on vacation from Cambridge, got his maiden century at the same time and we put on a record 251 for the fourth wicket. The record stand for the county had been set up by Close and Taylor three years before.

I earlier said the Weston wicket could be difficult. Well I had no obvious complaints as I belted my way confidently to my double century in just over three and a quarter hours.

The only trouble with the Clarence Park ground, as I find every year, is that every side of it—with its wall and high trees—looks the same. It's so easy to approach it by the wrong entrance.

Weston is usually full of Midland holiday-makers who come in off the beach when the sea goes out too far. It also has its great characters like Bill Andrews. Larger-than-life, extravagant in his well-intentioned claims, I've known no more loyal Somerset supporter. He'll tell you over a drink that he discovered most of the young Somerset players. And he probably did.

But sorry, Bill. Not even your far-reaching one-man scouting network got as far as St John's, Antigua!

So, overall, not a bad old season for I. V. A. Richards. A pity about that stupid game with Middlesex in the semi-final of the Gillette Cup. Can't you British do something about your weather? The two teams waited for six days and eventually we were forced to have a 15-over slog. We made a mess of it, as you may remember, and were all out for 59. Think of it! Three were run out; three more were out to full tosses. And Middlesex won in the 12th over. Brian Close looked on in helpless disgust as we destroyed ourselves. He was cussing violently under his breath. This, to a Yorkshireman, had nothing to do with cricket in any case. As a West Indian, I didn't think it had, either.

Miriam came over to England during the 1977 summer. She said she felt at home in Taunton straightaway. Some of my close friends had bought a welcoming bouquet for her. Soon she was admitting, 'It's almost like the West Indies, what with your stereo blaring away, Vivian.' Not that the climate had much similarity to Antigua and whenever Miriam began to shiver as she watched the cricket, my friends would warm her up with cups of tea. On one bitterly cold day at the county ground in Taunton I found her with my Somerset sweater wrapped tightly around her. Someone had found it for her.

The difficulty was always getting away from the crowds afterwards. But there were private moments—when we marvelled at the changes in our life, and shared an appreciative smile as we talked about good friends at home like 'Copper Head'. He's a member of the Cricket Association groundstaff and he often spots my car when, for instance, Miriam has driven it to work and left it outside the bank where she works. Unfailingly, this great guy called Copper Head gets hold of a bucket of water . . . and cleans the car. That's friendship for you.

Yes, quite a summer for me. I was by now seemingly established as a Test cricketer—as I'll be explaining later—and was topping the championship averages for Somerset for the first time.

Yet everything could have gone horrifyingly wrong for me on the M4 motorway. I'd driven up to Lord's with Pete McCombe to watch the final of the Benson and Hedges. We left before the end and there was no question that we'd had a couple of cans of beer too many. They were too warm for my taste, in any case. We called on my cousin, Ron Joseph, in London and then headed back for Taunton. It was early evening with not too much traffic on the road. I was cruising at 70 m.p.h. in my green Capri—and I had nothing on my mind. Pete had his seat down flat and was quietly snoring.

Suddenly we had a blow-out near the Newbury interchange. No chance to brake. It was scary, man. We were in the fast lane when it happened and fortunately there were no other cars alongside us at the time. My Capri careered towards the central crash barrier, spun round completely and shot right across the road. Then it went over the embankment on the near side and dropped a good twenty-feet—not on to grass but concrete. It all happened in a matter of seconds.

Pete was sleeping no longer. The two of us, shaking and

speechless, stumbled from the wrecked car. The wonder was that it was still the right way up. And, I suppose, that we were still alive. Neither of us had been wearing a seat belt.

Somehow we got back onto the motorway. Shock was setting in and I felt as though I'd got in the way of one of Andy Roberts' bouncers. Neither 'Jock' nor myself could blurt out many words. He claims that I straightened myself up and said, 'How do I look?' and that he burst out laughing at my supposed vanity. I don't remember what, if anything, I mumbled through my state of shock. I do know that the pair of us fainted on the spot before the ambulance arrived.

A police car came before the ambulance. There's something appealing about your cops, you know. This one took one of those cynical looks at my smashed car and then the trickles of blood all over Pete's face. He grinned at me and said, 'Just one thing before I take the details down—can I have your autograph, Viv?'

I expect I gave it to him. We were taken to hospital. I pulled a neck muscle but had survived pretty well unscathed. My passenger damaged his back, broke his nose and had a few nasty cuts about his head and face.

Growing up as I did the son of a prison officer, I've always been a law-and-order guy. Apart from boyish pranks up other people's fruit trees at home, I reckoned to keep the right side of the law. Let's forget that mad, midnight car chase in Bath. I wouldn't say a bad word about the cops. In Taunton I know most of them by sight anyway. We talk about cover drives and double yellows. Occasionally they string me along.

Like the one when I was motoring back from Canterbury in 1978 after our quarter final win against Kent. 'Jock' was also with me then—and was doing the driving. We never stayed late after away games. We liked to head for home; perhaps there might be a date waiting for me in Taunton.

I noticed when we passed through Maidstone that there was a patrol car parked at the lights. It began to follow us. Then it overtook us and signalled us to pull in. What was wrong? I hadn't been speeding and I wasn't over the top.

The cop walked back to us and leaned through the window.

He had that look about him which I couldn't quite place. I was in a hurry and didn't want any aggro.

'What have we done, then?' my driver asked.

I didn't really like the way he kept looking at me. Then he spoke. 'How did it finish today?'

He went on to explain that he'd been watching the Gillette tie on the telly but had to cut it short to go on duty.

We gave him a quick run-down and the Kent fan in a patrol car went sadly away. I suppose he's trained to recognise people. He certainly did a pretty good job on me as we went past him in a busy Maidstone street.

The 1978 season, light-hearted police scares apart, was a painful one for me. I so wanted to do well and help guide Somerset to their very first title. Somerset failed—and I failed when it mattered. My frustration boiled up in the final match at Taunton when I caused a stir by smashing my bat on the dressing room table. All in good (or bad) time. . . .

I was by now out of favour with my country because of my Packer employment. So it meant I could return promptly to Taunton and get on with it. I had a new three-year contract. My lawyer back in Antigua, Sidney Christian, who also looked after the affairs of Andy Roberts, had approved the small print as usual. Various clauses were written in. There was no unpleasant haggling with Somerset at any time. Life was beautiful. I had plenty of friends and warm letters from home. I was in the money and could occasionally be seen walking out of the county ground with a black business executive's briefcase in my hand. My wardrobe of good-quality shirts was increasing and I would spend up to £30 for a pair of shoes. The fish and chips in the shop just down the road from the county ground tasted as good as ever, but I could also get a bit more adventurous in my eating and didn't have to think twice about buying a gin-and-tonic or a brandy.

Having said that, I hated the trappings of success. I still got embarrassed when people paid me compliments in public. I wouldn't have my name plastered across the car that had been kindly given me. When I was invited to Ashton Gate to watch Bristol City play first division football I cringed if anyone said,

'Hey, this is Viv Richards', as if that was supposed to make it all right for me to have a free car park ticket.

At the county ground we had a new captain, Brian Rose, a left-hander who had played some very useful innings at the top of the order. I used to watch him quietly puffing away at his cigars between knocks and wondered how he'd make out. How much, I asked myself, had Brian Close's tough and wily qualities rubbed off on him?

When it became obvious that Closey was on the way, the speculation started about who would succeed him. Derek Taylor, who had been vice-captain, seemed the likeliest candidate. But he was coming up to his testimonial and had that on his mind. Pete Denning and Graham Burgess, the senior pro, were both mentioned. So, I noticed, was I.

I was never invited. That was hardly surprising when no-one really knew whether the dirty deed of joining Kerry Packer would put the permanent block on me as far as county cricket was concerned.

Would I have liked to captain Somerset? A West Country journalist friend asked me that in a private conversation. 'It's one thing skippering the West Indies, but something completely different leading a county side in England', I told him. 'I'm not sure I could have done it, what with the varying techniques required for one-day and three-day cricket. A Test series is brief. A season of county cricket is long, tiring and never easy for the captain.'

I'll come to the disappointments of the summer in a minute. There was a building atmosphere of success and we sensed that at last we were on to something. We didn't have to spell it out after every win but we'd sit on a Saturday morning, waiting to bat, and look at the championship table in the Daily Telegraph.

Rosey thought our best chance had to be in the one-day competitions. Until we lost our way against Kent and got a bit careless in August, I fancied the championship just as much. Everyone in the dressing room, as well as the president, Colin Atkinson and the chairman Roy Kerslake, was convinced we'd soon have a couple of pots on the shelf. A marketing firm was telling us how we ought to cash in.

89

The eyes of young, poorly-paid pros were sparkling at the prospect. I don't know if they were envious in some cases of my earnings from all sorts of sources. I sincerely hope not. I haven't changed as a person from the first time I entered the Taunton ground. That's the great thing about Hallam. Here's a fellow West Indian who bowled his big heart out for Somerset. He didn't play for his country although he probably deserved to. In the winter months, back in London with his family, he worked away on the building sites earning money to supplement his modest pay as a county cricketer. Often in the summer we shared digs and quiet moments. He knew me better than most— and must have realised I was suddenly a big earner. But not once was there a hint of envy. I hope he has a great testimonial in 1979 and I'll do what I can to help him.

I took a few weeks in 1978 to run into form. 'Too many late nights', Hallam joked. 'Balls!' I said. 'Too many problems with my feet at the moment.' Peter Robinson and I quickly put that right and the runs began to come.

By now I was more or less back to the fluent stroke-play that served me so well the previous summer and when I played for the West Indies, as well as Packer. July was a good month. Bill Alley put up his finger too quickly to have me out for 99 against Leicestershire at Taunton. But I got 114 in the second innings. As I've said before, I like to do well against that county!

Then came the visit of Warwickshire in the Gillette Cup. They thought they had us on the rack after scoring 292–5. We did it with nearly three overs to spare. It was the most runs ever scored in the Gillette Cup.

At various times through this eventful season we seemed to mismanage things at vital moments and create unnecessary problems for ourselves. I don't think 'Dredgy' and Vic Marks, the off-spinner who had captained Oxford University, would claim that they bowled particularly well against Warwickshire. Big Joel Garner was only half-fit and had to be nursed through his spells. They left us with one hell of a total to chase.

'Dasher' Denning gave us the right start with 60 and Peter Roebuck batted beautifully for 45. And I knew everyone was looking to me. I'd been more conscious of this responsibility over the last couple of months than ever before. 'You'll do it, Viv', the farmers used to say.

They didn't appear to accept that a player who likes to go for his shots all the time and can't resist the Big One now and again is liable to make a few mistakes.

But I grafted, man—how I grafted against Warwickshire. I've never worked harder. I kept one eye on the scoreboard and did my sums as I went along. Mathematics weren't my best subject back at the grammar school but I knew I needed five an over for most of the time. That meant I could push a little bit, and just give the bad one a licking. Trouble was there weren't many bad ones from the likes of Bob Willis.

I scored 139 not out and decided exactly where I'd put the winning hit—on to the roof of the pavilion. They made me Man of the Match . . . and we all had champagne afterwards.

There was another award for me in the semi-final against Essex at Taunton. If I play cricket in every country of the world, I'll never live through a more tense match. I pride myself on keeping my cool at the wicket but in this game my knees almost left me. Eleven runs were needed by Essex off the last over—and there was poor Colin Dredge nervously throwing in a no-ball. That final over took eight minutes and at the end the scores were level as Derek Taylor swooped like a goalkeeper to gather Brian Rose's oh-so gentle return for the vital run-out. We were through because we'd lost fewer wickets.

Earlier I'd been in good nick, leaning back to make space for myself to put Ray East away for six to extra cover. On the telly, Jim Laker said umpire Arthur Jepson had a look on his face which implied he'd never seen one like that before. I don't believe that. But it's a cheeky—and risky—sort of shot I like to try occasionally when I'm going well. 'Both' attempted to do the same later and didn't get away with it.

I was 94 not out at lunch and had the valued support of Peter Roebuck. We chatted away between overs and I tried to coax him along. Pete was getting anxious at one stage. The first 40 runs of our partnership hadn't produced one from him. I told him not to worry and he got the message. When his first came and the big crowd cheered with relief, Pete waved to them. I was

Right
With Ian Botham and
Peter Roebuck.

Below right
Autograph hunters can
be a pressure—not only
at Taunton! With
Miriam at Hove,
Sussex.

Below
The Richards:
with Barry after
our man-to-man
contest at Taunton,
September, 1978.

TAUNTON CIDER

out for 116 to the sort of brilliant catch at mid-wicket by Mike Denness that made me look twice.

It was too taut for comfort all through the Essex innings. I thought I had run-out Keith Fletcher before he had scored and he went on to make 67. I was used as an extra bowler and did a pretty good job until Keith Pont got at me. The closing overs were a nightmare, as the fielding got ragged and nervous shies at the wicket brought over-throws. We lost control badly and thought we had blown it. Back in the dressing room, the skipper said, 'I've aged a life-time.'

The atmosphere was magic. We were through to the final and my emotions ran away with me. It was an evening of sheer joy, as exciting as anything I had known as a Test cricketer. Ian Botham and myself stayed in the dressing room long after the others had left. We sat there with our couple of lagers, enjoying the moment. We took our time over the shower. Both of us knew, without having to say it, that we had come a long way since we kept each other awake at night in the club flat. It was ten o'clock before I left the ground.

Yet, as every red-faced, good-natured Somerset supporter will tell you, there was the bad scene of 1978, too. I had one or two 'down' moments before that dreadful climax when we lost the Gillette and the Sunday League in the same weekend.

It wasn't so funny, either, when I was sent back by the skipper and run-out without facing against Yorkshire in a Sunday match at Bristol's Imperial ground. Brian Rose and Peter Denning had made a solid start but we were well behind the clock and the crowd were getting edgy for runs. 'Put a sock in it, Viv', they said as I walked in. Not quite the expression I'm used to in Antigua but I got the gist. I immediately backed-up as Rosey pushed. Geoff Boycott hit the stumps with an under-arm throw—at my end. I hadn't even sensed the danger as I anticipated a simple run. Since then, I've kept my eye on the ball all the time. My slow-march back to the pavilion must have revealed how I was feeling. By the time Peter Walker snapped me out of it for a tea-time TV interview I was ready to agree that the run-out was my own fault. And it helped when I took a few wickets after that.

I can't make up my mind about Boycott. In that match he held himself back as the quick runs were badly needed and then surprisingly went in for the closing minutes. And he hit a lovely carefree six in the final over to suggest he could do it more often. His philosophy of occupying the crease at all costs, for most of the time, isn't my style. I've always reckoned anyone can do that if they don't play shots.

I had another brief 'down' during the Weston Festival. On the second day of the match with Warwickshire I wasn't in a good mood. I had a throbbing head. A cricketer knows when the runs aren't going to come. David Brown had me for six, even though it was a slightly lucky catch. Alvin Kallicharran, at first slip, couldn't retain the ball, and it spun off him, and Geoff Humpage the wicket keeper held on to it. I strolled back to the little Weston pavilion, curled up and went to sleep.

It hadn't been quite the forcing stuff I'd pulled out for my double century the previous year at Clarence Park.

Don't give me the old line that early nights are the only guarantee for a big score. I tried it before the Essex semi-final, scrapping a possible date and a few quiet drinks.

I was in bed by ten o'clock. And asleep by four or five in the morning! It was much too early for me. I wasn't sleepy and my head was buzzing with thoughts of clips off my pads for four and running catches at mid-wicket. When I did eventually fall off, it was almost time to get dressed. I arrived yawning at the ground and I daresay 'Breaky' and the others had the wrong idea.

Still I did try. And, after all, I made a century.

The first weekend in September was made for history. We knew we were the favourites for the Gillette Cup final and we talked over the tactics during the Friday night dinner in London. Chairman Roy Kerslake was with us. The composition of the team was uncertain with Phil Slocombe, Graham Burgess and Dennis Breakwell all fighting for one place.

In the end, the chairman and skipper opted for Budgie's experience and seam bowling. Phil, who must have nearly clinched it with several good recent innings and some tremendous fielding out on the boundary, was 12th man.

Dennis, who had scored his maiden century earlier in the

summer against the New Zealanders and was proving himself a genuine allrounder, can blame his injuries for being left out.

We played it badly and lost. We feared the 207–7 wouldn't be quite enough and Sussex, who on paper didn't have a chance, won it with 41 balls left. 'Both' hit a typically spunky 80.

We had to parade on the balcony at Lord's at the end for our losers' medals and all we wanted to do was slink away. Down below, 4,000 Somerset supporters hoisted banners like 'Richards walks on scrumpy.' I was in no mood to smile back.

Inside again, away from the fans we felt we'd let down, I squeezed my losers' medal and hurled it on to the floor. I never wanted to see it again.

I understand that 'Dasher' later picked it up and passed it on to a friend. He can keep it. I want nothing to commemorate failure.

Depression lifted and we said, 'One down, one to go.'

I think it was 'Both' who said, 'We'll cane those buggers tomorrow.'

I showered and climbed into my car. I was back in Taunton by half past ten. Not to bed straightaway—but nothing mad, either.

We only needed to tie with Essex on the Sunday to be sure of the John Player League. If Hampshire beat Middlesex, we'd still win on run rate.

Stay-at-home television addicts were probably sick of seeing us on the box. But they must have been amazed at the kind of support we had that afternoon. I have never seen as many at the Taunton ground. They were sitting on the top of the stands and up in the trees and you could almost smell the apple juice. They were as happily noisy as any crowd I've known at Port of Spain or Georgetown or Kingston. It was a fabulous kind of support and some of the younger players were visibly affected by it as they laced their boots.

We lost again. Essex were allowed to make too many, 190–5. And we failed by two runs as Keith Jennings and Hallam tried for an impossible third extra off the last ball.

It was the one game in which I was going to excel. Talk about motivation—I had never worked harder to will myself to get a lot of runs. This was my county and I was going to win something for them. It didn't help that the fans were shouting about 'another ton' from me as I walked to the wicket. They honestly expected too much from me that season and the pressure was getting at me. My first five scoring strokes were fours and the crowd were cheering everything. And then I changed my mind. I was going to play Graham Gooch off my pads for a comfortably lofted four but I drew back and decided for a single so that I could keep the bowling. In horror, I watched the ball go down Brian Hardie's throat.

I find it hard to put down on paper what happened at the end of this agonising match, while the loyal, sympathetic Somerset supporters continued to cheer us as if we had won. It's still too painful.

There we were, slumped around the benches. Grown men were crying like kids. I was in tears. So was 'Both'. And Vic Marks and Keith Jennings. I expect others were but I didn't notice them.

To me it was unbearable. I was bitterly sorry for the team. I was angry for myself. Suddenly the sheer frustration of being so near a title two days running exploded for me.

Hardly knowing what I was doing I walked away from the others, my favourite, trusted 'Jumbo' bat in my hand. I got as far as the area around the showers and in one uncontrollable gesture I brought the bat down on the stone floor. It broke and splintered in my hand.

I left the bat in pieces on the floor.

That lousy defeat on a sunny Taunton evening, in front of ten thousand fans who would have followed us to the ends of the earth, was the worst moment of my life.

Cricket is emotional as far as I'm concerned. In that varied and mostly successful 1978 summer I'd lived through joy at as high a peak as I've ever experienced in cricket. And now, in that weeping dressing-room, I was near despair.

The crowd were still calling and we dutifully made a brief appearance on the balcony. They were bloody marvels. And it made everything a million times more painful.

I turned to a friend later that night, when I was able to think straight again, and said, 'Do you know, I can't think of anything worse, except a death in the family.'

We stayed in that dressing room for 45 minutes. For most of that time we were silent. What was there to say, anyway? The doors were bolted so that no-one would come in. We couldn't even face the committeemen who wanted to sympathise.

Gradually we managed a wry grin as we bathed and changed. Once more the last two left there were Ian Botham and myself. We were joined by a crestfallen Roy Kerslake and the former Somerset off-spinner Brian Langford. For a long, long time we stayed shaking our heads as we gulped the beer. Where had it all gone wrong? We had the best side in the country—and there wasn't a damned thing to show for it.

There were plans for a celebration reception in Taunton on the Monday and a ride in an open-top bus through the streets of Bridgwater and Weston-super-Mare. HTV were intending us to have lunch in Weston at the Grand Atlantic Hotel and then drive us triumphantly to their studios for a live appearance in the 6 o'clock News programme. Suddenly we didn't want to know. We knew there could be no bus-rides now. Everything had gone unbelievably sour.

If there had been a plane leaving Bristol Airport for Coolidge, Antigua, in half an hour I'd have been on it. At least, that's how I felt as I slumped, my head in my hands, re-living the dolly catch to mid-wicket a hundred times.

The season was over for me, apart from a mid-September challenge match against Barry Richards at Taunton for a £1,000 wager. I was feeling pretty shattered and missed the last county fixture, against Worcestershire. My doctor gave me a thorough four-hour check up. Two years earlier I'd gone to Frenchay Hospital near Bristol because of sinus and other minor trouble.

The two defeats, against Sussex and Essex, however, had left me jaded. I didn't want to talk cricket with the fans I met in the Taunton streets or when I played pool at the Gardeners Arms. Most players feel at some time like a complete break from the game. In my case, I'd been hitting a cricket ball all the year round since 1974.

*   *   *

However much I enjoy the life—and the perks that go with it—I admit that there are moments when, psychologically, it gets on top of me. I feel I want to curl up in a corner of my flat listening to my music, or retreating miles from the nearest cricket ground with a few friends and a few cans of lager.

I know that I was looking just a bit stale when I returned to Somerset for the start of the 1978 season. I had a contract to honour—but I'd have jumped at the chance of another month away from the game. As the summer went on, of course, I quickly regained my appetite, although I asked for a rest against the New Zealanders. I don't know if any of my teammates sensed how tired I was in those early matches. Certainly my reflexes were sluggish by my own demanding standards.

Jaded or not early on, depressed or not at the end of the season as the titles slipped away, I left Somerset in late summer with a couple of happy sporting memories.

The £1,000 winner-take-all challenge match with Barry Richards that I've mentioned was quite a success. Perhaps I should explain that I won!

Barry and I were supposedly the two best batsmen in the world—at least that was what the match publicity claimed. The idea had come from a local marketing man Mike Taylor who was helping with Derek Taylor's (no relation) testimonial. He'd sensed that Barry was losing interest in county cricket and that one of the remaining incentives was money. When the idea was first mooted, I understand Barry wasn't too enthusiastic.

My own reaction when I was asked whether I'd play for £1,000 was, 'Sure!'

Taunton Cider Company generously came up with the sponsorship and it was agreed that Derek Taylor would get the net profits from the gate. Various bonuses were carefully worked out for boundaries—and the bowlers and fielders weren't forgotten.

By the time the match was played Barry had left Hampshire with not too much sign of mutual affection, it seemed to me.

He flew over specially from New York to attend the photocall on the Friday before our Sunday game. There were photographers and camera crews everywhere. This apparently unique idea of two international cricketers pitting their skills—and their wallets—against each other had tickled the fancy of the public.

In between one session with the photographers out on the pitch and a television interview lined up for the early afternoon, I escaped with a few friends to the Ring of Bells down the road. 'I've never known anything like this—give me some freedom', I whispered. I wasn't enjoying the hassle.

But after a gobbled salad and pickled onions it was back to the ground for more publicity. Then I had to drive to Bristol for another TV interview, this time live.

Who am I to complain, I suppose you could say, when I'm playing for £1,000-plus in an afternoon?

One or two people, with maybe a thought for a future headline to boost the crowd, suggested it was quite a grudge match. White South African against black West Indian, I imagine they meant. That line made no impression on me. Barry was someone I rated as a cricketer—and that was the only yardstick I was interested in. Andy Roberts, who had played with him for Hampshire, had gone home after the various English seasons and told me how stylish this opening bat was. I'd played against him, of course, and although he didn't always come off against Somerset he'd done enough to remind me of his exceptional skills.

Five thousand spectators watched our match. We both faced 25 overs and the number of runs was divided by the dismissals. My average was 68 and Barry's was just over 38.

Some cynical cricket fans had anticipated it would be a gimmicky contest. They were wrong. We both tried desperately to win.

In the end I picked up the top cash prize and the solid silver trophy. Between us, Barry and I also pocketed £230, based on the number of boundaries. And Derek Taylor was also smiling. He took all the net gate money, about £3,000.

*   *   *

The county cricketer in England copes with one hell of a schedule. He travels from one side of the country to the other, often late at night, to be ready for the next fixture. The one-day matches have put the kind of physical and mental strain on him that few members of the public appreciate.

And then there are the benefit games. As I quickly discovered, professional cricketers show a loyalty to each other. I think my record of attendance for the dozens of testimonial matches since I became a Somerset player is as good as anyone in the club.

Beneficiaries are apt to say, 'Hope you can make it tomorrow night, Viv. They all want to see you play.'

'A man short again?' I joke.

My first appearance in a testimonial game was for Mervyn Kitchen, even before I'd officially joined Somerset. After that came regular matches in turn for Peter Robinson, now the coach, Tom Cartwright, Graham Burgess and Derek Taylor. And obviously I'll be doing my best for Hallam Moseley in 1979. There's one big omission in the list—Brian Close. I was always his No. 1 fan and would have willingly turned out for him in 1976. But that was the summer when West Indies cricket kept me away from Somerset altogether.

I can tell you one thing. My experiences playing in testimonial games left me with a knowledge of by-ways and country lanes that made me think I knew rural Somerset as well as inland Antigua.

But, man, I learned the hard way. I was getting lost all the time as I hunted for little villages that weren't even in the AA book.

The beneficiaries would painstakingly give me instructions. These weren't reliable all the time. And they never seemed to warn me about the broken-down signposts and large herds of cows which held me up for ten minutes as they stumbled home at milking time.

Some of my pronunciations, too, of words like Huish Episcopi and Nempnett Thrubwell apparently had more of a Caribbean than a West Country ring to them. Come to think of it, I couldn't exactly understand what the old mid-Somerset farmers were saying, either. I've never quite managed to come to terms with the local accent which appears to get more and more broad with every pint washed down.

Once or twice I arrived at the wrong village—and the wrong ground. The locals must have wondered what a young black man was doing looking over a gate at an empty sports field covered with buttercups. If I arrived late it wasn't necessarily my fault. Honestly. Other members of the Somerset team, with voices that at least belonged to the area, did the same.

There was a match for Derek Taylor's benefit in the South Somerset village of North Perrott, I remember. The trouble was that we were invited to a luncheon given by a leading cider company in Norton Fitzwarren first. The two villages must be 25 miles apart—across country.

It was, I should say, a good lunch. We were encouraged to sample the apple juice.

Eventually we got away, having all agreed that there was no cider better than Somerset's. We set off in some sort of convoy but that arrangement didn't last for long. Some of the drivers weren't too sure what time the North Perrott match was due to start—but we all knew we were cutting it pretty fine.

It didn't bother me too much. Time never has. If we arrange to see a few friends in St John's, we're apt to say 'See you in the afternoon' rather than 'See you at half past two.' There's nothing wrong with a wrist watch as long as we don't look at it too often. But in England you are more concerned about such things. And I expect the villagers at North Perrott were, as they waited for the county cricketers to arrive.

Fortunately our team that afternoon was being made up by a few loyal camp followers. They included Ivor Salter, a Taunton television actor who loves his cricket and plays the occasional match for us when he is 'resting'.

When we arrived at the pretty little ground, Ivor and a colleague were already doing their stuff. They were out in the middle, stone-walling.

Perhaps it wasn't exactly festival cricket for a few overs. But they knew they had to stay there until the rest of the team turned up. Between every shot, they looked anxiously towards the entrance. I know what they must have felt like when the line of cars arrived. We changed quicker than we had ever done before, juggled with the batting order, depending on the first to tie their boots, and had a very pleasant game. No-one worried too much. We complimented Ivor on his straight-down-the-line exhibition . . . and promised we'd watch his next TV play.

Testimonial matches can be quite relaxing. There's an absence of pressure—and unexpected talents are often revealed. Opening batsmen turn into bowlers and stumper Derek Taylor shows off his off-breaks.

Although these afternoon and evening matches on strange village wickets can be fun, I'm against anything that can be considered gimmicky. I don't believe that professional cricketers should ever risk making a fool of themselves in public.

Let me give just one example. We went to a nice village ground, West Pennard, somewhere between Glastonbury and Shepton Mallet. During the tea interval, Derek asked me if I would take part in an unusual challenge. The idea was to see how far I could hit a cricket ball in relation to a golf ball.

The golfer was Gordon Brand, a promising young player from Bristol very much on the way up in the game. He had arrived with his clubs and was taking a few practice swings outside the pavilion. A press photographer was waiting to record the unique event. Allowances over distance were to be made in my favour.

That challenge match never took place. The young golfer and the press photographer went home puzzled.

I refused to take part. I did it as tactfully as I could. There was no bad feeling.

But that kind of contest was not for me. It seemed a ridiculous way to measure one skill against another. And I argued that I could easily risk injury if I took an almighty swing in such an unnatural situation.

One or two, I expect, thought it was churlish of me.

Derek didn't insist. He was perhaps disappointed, particularly after persuading young Gordon Brand to motor down to West Pennard.

That village match, in the August of 1978, holds one or two other memories for me. It got off to a slightly embarrassing start when a rather pompous spectator started to go for me because I had refused earlier to sign an autograph for a boy. He got his facts wrong—and his belligerent manner privately upset me.

I have my own set of rules for dealing with autograph-hunters. If I am with someone, involved in a conversation, I ask the boys to wait till later. On this afternoon I had already asked a dozen or so boys if, because I was having a private chat with a friend on the boundary before going in to bat, they would ask me again later.

I did it, as usual, quietly and politely. I think the man who strode up to me was a parent. He appeared to be ready for an argument. My friend cut him short in mid-sentence by explaining what had happened.

The signing of autographs can be a bind. Few cricketers, coming tired and perhaps dejected from the field, want to be bothered by a circle of small boys, brandishing their books and photographs. It's true that some players are better than others. Maybe they have more patience. Hallam must be the best in Somerset. I'm not as patient as that but I realise we owe it to the kids who support the game and treat us as their heroes. I love children and dutifully sign their autograph books. But, I insist, at the right time.

I remember once when I was playing for the West Indies at Lord's. After the game scores of youngsters were hanging round in anticipation of a few prized signatures. As usual, I was taking my time in the shower. I think the main reason I do this is that sub-consciously I hope the crowd will have gone home by the time I emerge. That, I promise you, isn't arrogance or contempt for the public who have been good enough to pay to see me play. It's basic shyness. Despite my widening experience I'll never completely change.

At Lord's that evening, long after the final ball, I was told a visitor was waiting to see me. He was Terry Harding, one of my old friends from Lansdown C.C. We had a few idle words about the match and then Terry said:

'Hate to bother you, Viv. But I have a young lad here at the game. He's come all the way down from Yorkshire to get your autograph.'

It was a genuine sob-story and I couldn't ignore it from a bloke from Bath. Out I went, met the lad and signed his book.

Within minutes I was signing for fifty or more of them. There was no escape. 'Never again', I swore to myself.

I also get slightly cross when I'm taken for a ride, even by a boy. I've no time for those who pester you . . . so that they can then sell your signature. Once at the county ground in Bristol, a couple of lads rushed up to me and said, 'Can we have your autograph, Viv?'

My response was to give them a long critical look. I've got a useful memory for faces.

'Not on your life', I said. 'I signed for you last night.'

They knew I was right and moved away sheepishly.

The incident at West Pennard illustrates the problem for the professional sportsman.

I said that was quite an eventful testimonial match. During my innings I hit a ball hard back over the bowler. One of the well-known village cricketers, Peter Bolton, tried to stop the six. The force of the ball took him back against a barbed-wire fence. He lost his balance and went head-first over the top. His flannels caught in the wire and there he remained, suspended with feet dangling helplessly in the air for up to five minutes while the rest of the players tried to disentangle him. They were afraid he was badly cut but he survived with a few scratches on his legs.

'Always an ambition of mine to catch Viv Richards', he joked afterwards. A painful way of attempting it, Peter.

Cricket, you'll gather, isn't really a laughing matter for me. All the same, I've joined in a few harmless pranks during the testimonial matches.

In a game at Exeter for 'Budgie' Burgess, when I was keeping wicket, we decided to fake a catch. The ball didn't leave the bowler's hand—because he didn't have it in the first place. I'd kept it in my gloves and at the appropriate moment I threw it triumphantly into the air for a catch. Everyone appealed. The batsman knew what was happening, entered into the spirit and walked. I'm sure it confused some of the Devon spectators.

Peter Roebuck is one of the 'thinkers' of our county side. So he should be with that law degree. He stands there in his spectacles, working out his theories. One, I think, is that you can kid the umpire if you stage-manage your ploy carefully enough.

He decided to try it out during a testimonial game in mid-Somerset. After the fifth ball of an over, we all changed-over. We did it with straight faces, looking at the umpire out of the corner of our eyes. He obviously came to the conclusion that we must be right and eventually called 'Over'.

I'm not sure we'd get away with that in a first-class match, of course.

With the West Indies

It must be something about the West Indian temperament that allows us to take surprises in our stride. But on the afternoon during the Bath cricket festival in 1974 when a reporter from the Bristol Evening Post broke the news to me that I'd been chosen for the West Indies tour of India, Sri Lanka and Pakistan my legs caved in.

Quite honestly I didn't think I had the remotest chance. I was still in my first season with Somerset getting the feel of professional cricket and gradually making the transition to a different ball game—different that is, from St John's, Rising Sun and Lansdown. This wasn't week-end cricket—and a can of lager afterwards as the funk music was spun on the jukebox.

Somerset's Brian Close apparently liked the look of me. I was acquiring more discipline at the crease, playing better off the front foot and often keeping the ball on the ground. I was beginning to feel more like a cricketer. I had a natural sense of timing—and a powerful pair of shoulders. They were two loyal allies.

But Test cricket? Not a chance. My record at home, where it really counted as far as the selectors were concerned, meant nothing at top class level. I'd gone off to Bath and they heard little about me for one whole summer. And who, after all, was interested in this lad from Antigua who was said to like his soccer just as much as his cricket?

In fact, my father, Malcolm Richards, still probably meant more to them as a name. He had been a big-hearted fast bowler, doing his stuff for my island in the zone games. Three of his sons had played for Antigua, too. But it was unthinkable that one of them, Vivian, just 22, would go on a Test tour.

I stumbled out some sort of incoherent reaction to the sports reporter from Bristol and then I heard the loudspeaker announcement made around the ground. Soon black, smiling faces, friends who had known me when I lodged in the city, were surrounding me with congratulations. I was too numb to take it in.

That night Mr Creed took me off for a celebration drink. And the more I thought about it, the more I was convinced that the selectors had boobed. I just didn't think I was ready for it. I mentally went through the names of some of the great West Indians I'd be travelling with. It scared the hell out of me.

The tour party flew out and I was pretty subdued. It was Andy Roberts's first tour, too, and we stuck together. We dutifully attended the receptions although we'd have opted for something less formal. They took us to view the Taj Mahal but I wasn't in a position to grasp what was happening to me. Everything was unreal. I was surrounded by great West Indian cricketers and I felt the new boy. I reckoned I should have been asking for their autographs rather than buckling on my pads alongside them.

It didn't exactly help when I flopped in my first Test against India. We won by 267 runs—and I was out for 4 and 3. Chandrasekhar got me both times. I holed-out to extra cover and then mis-read the spin to snick a simple catch to gully.

That was also Gordon Greenidge's first Test. At least he did something about it. Gordon confidently made 107 in the second innings.

I won't start trying to tell you how down I was. Back in the dressing room I slumped on the bench and came to a definite conclusion: Test cricket was too hard for me. I wasn't up to it. I'd been found out at that level. My own fears that I was nothing like ready for international cricket were being confirmed.

I remember Clive Lloyd, Deryck Murray and Roy Fredericks coming up to me as I sat dejectedly on my own. They tried to console me. They said, 'Snap out of it, Vivi. You'll make it!'

I can still see them saying it to me. They did their best to lift me. And so did off-spinner Albert Padmore by his sense of

107

Above Someone I admire enormously—Mike Procter.
Below 3rd Test, England v. West Indies at Old Trafford 1976. What courage!
Brian Close ducks another bouncer from Michael Holding. I am at short leg.

humour. Here was a great character to have in any tour party. He took the mickey out of all the players. He was effervescent and good-natured. Albert never cared what he said. And he could end the tensest of situations with one of his highly personal remarks.

Several of the more experienced players took me on one side. 'You're not rushing to catch the next plane at Coolidge. Don't try to belt every ball out of sight. Just curb it a bit.'

I smiled to myself, hearing Clive telling me to steady it. I've seen some fantastic innings from him for the West Indies. Talk about a rush!

In fact, he had a fine tour, finishing easily top of the batting averages and often murdering the Indian spinners. He was apt to live dangerously. But with his reach and magnificent striking skill he could demoralise an opposing side like no other cricketer I have ever seen.

There was one consolation for me in that maiden Test. I took the catch which I believe will remain my best.

I was fielding at short-leg to Van Holder and the batsman was Gavaskar. The ball was a short one and it was really whacked off the blade. There wasn't too much time to think about ducking. In fact, it was going just behind me as I crouched. Instinctively I dived backwards and the ball stuck between two fingers.

That day I also caught the other Indian opener, Farokh Engineer, off Andy Roberts. Two catches went no way at all, however, towards offsetting the miserable exhibitions I'd given at the wicket.

Centuries in a couple of minor matches at Poona and Jullunder didn't kid me. I had to prove myself in the next Test or accept the fact that my future was unlikely to rise above county cricket in England.

The pitch at Delhi was slow and none too reliable. The Indian spinners had a psychological advantage even though we'd got on top in the first Test.

We won by an innings. And I made it. Clive Lloyd sent me in at No. 5 and I scored 192 not out. I believe that if I'd failed again in that match I'd have been resigned to an abrupt end to a brief Test career.

I was very nervous when I went in. I tried to remember what I was advised on how to face the spinners. Then I started to enjoy myself with six sixes and twenty fours. At the other end, Clive swung his bat beautifully.

There were a few murmurs from the Indians afterwards. They seemed to think I was caught at the wicket when I'd scored 12. They were equally sure Keith Boyce had been caught at slip before he was off the mark. I had no doubts in my mind.

India played themselves back into the series with two wins and we all got a bit anxious when it came to the decider. We won by 201 runs; Lance Gibbs bowled on a lovely length to take 7–98 in the first innings and Van Holder took a vital 6–39 in the second.

Who'll forget Clive Lloyd's double century in the match? Or the ugly crowd scenes that marked it? As you'll recall I've found myself bang in the middle of the odd riot. But this was my first experience of trouble in India. The police seemed altogether too heavy-handed in dealing with the spectators who ran on the field to congratulate Clive. I don't know what possessed them—they went wild. They started swinging their bamboo canes and it was their lack of judgment, for all to see, which incited the crowd. The pitch was quickly littered with missiles and rubbish and there were anxious meetings between State ministers and the cricket officials. We lost 90 minutes play because of it on the second day and when we asked the Indian Board to make it up, they said No. We didn't think much of that decision.

It meant that the West Indies had to go for very quick runs in the second innings. I flung my bat for 39 off 23 balls. The skipper hit 37 off 17 balls. Earlier in the game there had been a lovely century from Roy Fredericks. And we did it—riots or not.

I expect there would have been a few questions asked at home if we'd thrown the series away after winning the first two Tests. But there were no recriminations after the way we eventually clinched it. Clearly we were still unpredictable and we proved it again by being bowled out for 119 in our second match against Sri Lanka. It was the lowest score ever made by a Test side there. We weren't very proud of that one.

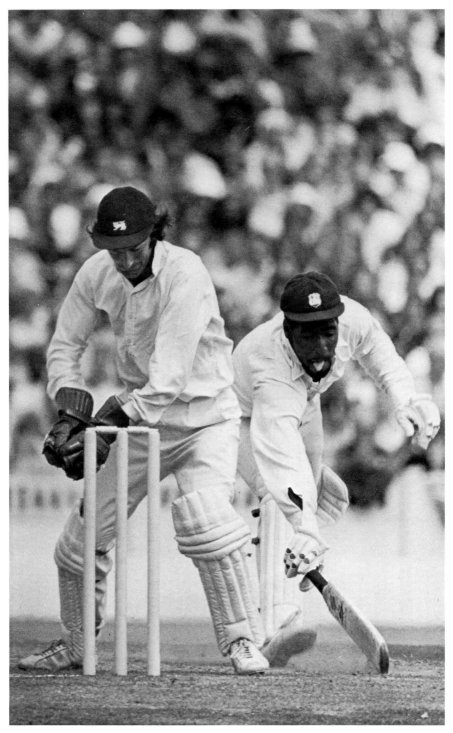

3rd Test, England v. West Indies at Old Trafford 1976.
A close thing—Alan Knott is wicket keeper.

All the travelling left me in a daze. I don't like going by plane, anyway. I hate living from a suitcase. Still the two Tests against Pakistan to come—and I couldn't wait to get home. The glamour of representing my country was starting to pale just a little.

At Lahore I didn't do myself much good by being out for 7 and 0. The match was drawn and one of the encouraging things to emerge was a not-out century by Len Baichan in his first Test for us.

We also drew the second Test, at Karachi. I have some pretty vivid memories of that match, not much to do with my own contribution. There were plenty of runs around—centuries by Majid Khan and Wasim Raja for Pakistan, Kallicharran and Bernard Julian, batting at No 7, for us. Kalli had pulled out some lovely innings during the series and I envied his style.

I also remember the courage of Sadiq Mohammed, the Gloucestershire opener, at Karachi. He was fielding at short leg (in the pre-helmet days) to Bernard when our man was really breezing along. Sadiq was badly hit in the face. He still carried his bat for 98 later in the game. That was one of the two best knocks I've ever seen from him. The other was in the Sunday League against Somerset.

It wasn't only Sadiq who needed pluck in that Test. The worst crowd scenes I've ever experienced occurred when some spectators ran on to the pitch to congratulate their idol Wasim Raja after he'd got his ton. Then came the police.

'Hello', I said to myself, 'I've seen all this before in India. I'm getting off.'

As the pitch was quickly invaded on all sides, the West Indian boys made for cover. We watched what was going on almost in disbelief. I wouldn't like to guess how many were hurt as the police batons were raised. The spectators themselves went wild. It was absolute chaos. Two and a half hours of play were lost on this second day of the final Test. Some of us didn't think that the cricket would ever start again.

I had time to ponder—either on the plane between venues, or waiting for the riots to stop. So this was Test cricket in the Seventies. . . .

In my quiet way I was building up friendships with the other West Indian cricketers. I was glad for Andy—he had taken 44 Test wickets, which must be a terrific way to make your mark on your first tour.

There were one or two off-the-field dramas. Roy Fredericks actually asked for his ticket home at one stage.

He was often in great form with the bat and scored one double century against Combined Universities as well as two hundred in the Tests. But in a match in Pakistan he was given out twice for LBW. The umpire's decision, at least in one case, was laughable. Roy was well outside the leg stump when the ball hit his pads. A blind man wouldn't have given him out.

This umpire did—to the surprise of most of the fielders and the less partisan members of the crowd. Roy was mad. He went to see our manager Gerry Alexander and asked for his ticket home and his passport.

'I don't want to stay out here. There are better umpires back in Berbice, Guyana where I was born.'

I'm sure there were. All the time we were coming up against bad umpiring standards. Why, Lance Gibbs was no-balled for the first time in his career. There was fury in his eyes.

The likelihood of getting their batsmen LBW was remote. Lance Gibbs once had a Pakistan player plumb in front. Nothing could have been clearer. Everyone appealed. The umpire looked away.

The bowler was disgusted. When it came to the next over, he very deliberately took off his floppy hat as if to hand it to the umpire. At the last moment he pulled his hand away and stuffed the hat in his own pocket.

He was saying, in effect, 'I wouldn't even trust you to hold my hat for me.'

I don't know what I really expected from Test cricket— outside the cricket, that is.

Socially, India, Sri Lanka and Pakistan weren't the height of exciting action.

'Australia's different. It swings out there,' the lads were saying as they packed their bags for the last time in Karachi.

That's all right if you're still in the team, I thought to myself. I

Keep watching the ball.

wasn't at all sure that I'd made the impact I should have.

But I was in . . . The tour came earlier than expected. The Aussies had cancelled their tour of South Africa and we went out to give them a series. Perhaps we should have stayed at home. We lost 5–1.

There was a lot of criticism of us on that tour. Not so much for lack of discipline off the field as lack of temperament on it. We failed too often when the crunch was on.

Of course, we'd never won a series in Australia. But the way we won the second Test at Perth by an innings on a fast wicket which suited us perfectly made us think we might be changing the pattern. It was a painfully false impression.

We should have done better. At times we gave our wickets away as though we were bent on self-destruction. Yet we had Mike Holding bowling perhaps faster than anyone in the world, more fiery than Thommo and Lillee. And we had Lance Gibbs on his last tour and on the verge of taking more wickets than Freddie Trueman in Test cricket.

Lance, a wonderful bowler, did it eventually in the final sixth Test at Melbourne. Everyone was willing him to succeed. Mike Holding grimly held on to the catch and Freddie's great record of 307 victims had gone.

My own tour was patchy. I was soon heading for a bout of the depressions, in fact, when Lillee got me for a duck in the first Test. It didn't help much when I ran myself out in the second innings for 12. No, I don't wish to remember that match at Brisbane.

I made five centuries while I was out there but only one really counted in my book. The 175 against Western Australia at Perth should have put me right as it came immediately before the second Test, but it didn't. I took two hundreds off Tasmania at Hobart and one against Western New South Wales Country XI at Dubbo. Some of the bowling was pretty benevolent. It was in the Tests that I needed to turn it on.

Morale, I recall, was suspect after we'd been caned by seven wickets in the fourth Test. They sent me in first for a minor tour match and I rattled a fairly confident 93. When it came to Adelaide and the fifth Test I was opening with Roy Fredericks.

The last two Tests, when I went in first, were my best of the series. I scored 30 and 101, before Lillee got me, in the Adelaide match, and 50 and 98 at Melbourne. I think the added responsibilities were right for me then. It was a canny move and I responded successfully, I feel. During our stay in Australia I'd run into a few technical problems while I was batting. Andy Roberts, looking at me through a bowler's eyes, detected where I was partly going wrong. Funny that it takes a bowler to spot it. I couldn't get things right and was getting myself out unnecessarily. It was all a matter of having my feet in the correct place for the shot. But the difficulty of conditioning myself to Australian wickets after those in England was there for all to see. West Indian Test players who spend their summers in England all have this problem acclimatising themselves when they move abruptly from one kind of wicket to another.

It was an edgy tour. We knew we weren't doing well enough and we read the reports that Esmond Kentish and Keith Walcott weren't supposedly strict enough.

The first tour of Australia must be the height of ambition for any young cricketer. We went out so full of promise, even though some of us were a bit stale through too many matches.

And, in the end, all we had to show for it was that runaway and deceptive win at Perth. Andy bowled beautifully there to take 7–54 in the second innings. I'll remember for years the big scoring of Ian Chappell—one of his great innings, I'm assured—Clive Lloyd and Roy Fredericks. Roy's knock of 169 was incredible for the way he kept hooking the fast bowlers. His timing and courage were tremendous. The more the Aussies pitched short, the more he put them away.

On this tour I faced Jeff Thomson for the first time. He was the fastest I'd come up against at that time. He made them whistle down at you—and you relied on your eyes, your feet and a silent prayer.

There's a good deal talked about hostile bowlers and intimidation. I hope it doesn't sound arrogant to say I don't mind who I'm facing out there in the middle—fast or slow. It's one against one and on average the bowler is more likely to let go

4th Test, England v. West Indies at Headingley 1976.
Above Peter Willey is the fielder in the background—he seems to be enjoying himself!
Below The end. Bob Willis gets me.

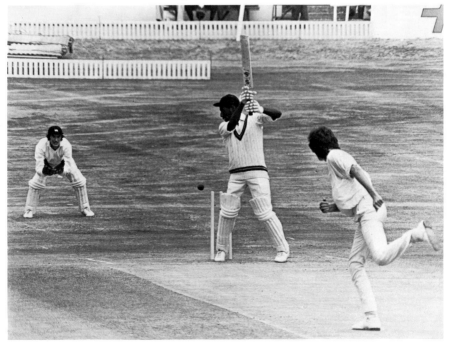

a bad ball than the batsman is to play a bad stroke.

Which do I prefer, quickies or spinners? The question is always being asked me in Antigua, Andover and Adelaide. I have no special liking—or fear—of any. Provided, as I've spelt out so often in this book, the wicket is reliable and true.

The strips are so much faster at home that West Indians have an advantage in standing up to the pace bowlers.

I hope I shall never in my cricketing life be accused of flinching. Bad-tempered fast bowlers can pitch them short at me as much as they like. I'll accept the challenge. That means getting my feet right for the hook. Short-pitched balls can be punished. They can be a bonus to the batsman.

I've taken a few blows in the process. Thommo once cracked me on the jaw during that West Indies tour of Australia. I rubbed it hard and went on batting. At the end of the day my jaw and neck had swelled up as if I had the mumps.

And here's a confession. Until I came to England I never used to wear a box. Put it down to the sharp eye, the confidence and perhaps the folly of youth.

Thank God I was wearing one when Len Pascoe caught me in that vulnerable region. I've never been so grateful in my life.

The force of the delivery demolished my box—but I survived!

Unlike many professional cricketers I wear a minimum of protective clothing when I go to the wicket. Just a thigh guard and a box, in fact.

I have never contemplated wearing a helmet. After that vicious knock he got on the face when fielding at short leg in Pakistan, for instance, I don't blame Sadiq wearing a helmet. It should be the choice of the players.

My personal view, however, is that a helmet with a visor takes a little of the batsman's vision—and just a little of the challenge out of the game.

Obviously if you're facing Thommo or Dennis Lillee, Andy or Mike Holding every other day on a hard wicket with some bounce, you don't relax your concentration too often. That means, I suppose, that you shouldn't have a late night before you walk up to stare them out down the wicket.

The night before the West Indies played New South Wales, I

remember, I had a few drinks. Perhaps rather more than a few. When, next morning, I stood up to David Colley my reflexes were more sluggish than they should have been. He hit me on the top of the head. It was my own fault.

I have to admit that Australia was more to my liking in the social sense. I didn't need a lot of persuading to return there to play for Queensland for three months. I had signed a contract for David Lord to handle my affairs out there. Thommo and Alvin Kallicharran were also on his books. He got me the contract to play for Queensland and I linked up with the radio station 41P.

Apart from commitments to the station, there were commercial considerations. We launched a new beer for instance. Equally happily, Thommo and myself went out to some of the State schools and coached the kids.

There were, as I've indicated, one or two complications when Mr Lord wanted me to ditch Packer. Later I wrote to him and asked to be withdrawn from any obligations with him. The parting was fairly friendly.

I played four Sheffield Shield games for Queensland under Greg Chappell and also took part in a bit of grade cricket. The social life appealed almost as much as the matches. Remember I was still only 24 and life—and friendships—were opening up to me.

I had a big car on hire while I was out there. On the last night in Australia I was returning from a party in the early hours. My speed must have been 120 mph. And an Australian cop didn't approve, rightly so.

He stopped me and pulled out his notebook.

Like the one I tangled with on the way home from Canterbury, this Australian policeman took a long, hard look at me.

'You're Vivian Richards, aren't you?'

'That's right.'

'Sorry, Vivian, but I've got to book you.'

'But I'm leaving—'

'Leaving Australia? When?'

'Tomorrow.'

In full cry at The Oval.

With that he grinned and put his book away.

'Not much I can do then, is there.'

A public face can help, I suppose. The Avon and Somerset Constabulary weren't quite as sports-minded. My licence bears just one endorsement—for speeding home to Taunton after a match at Bath.

Delhi, Calcutta, Madras, Sri Lanka, Lahore, Karachi, Perth, Adelaide, Sydney, Brisbane . . . I was finding it difficult to absorb what was happening to me. Because I had seemingly some natural ability to hit a small red ball hard and often and because with a freakish bit of luck I had been brought to England and given a chance, I was now flying round the world. Countries that had never meant any more to me than a vague mention in geography classes at the grammar school were suddenly there for the taking. I should probably have studied them more intently when I landed. But as I tumbled out of aircraft, with my baggage and my tired jet-eyes, I didn't want too much culture and education. And I expect most of my teammates felt the same way.

Don't ask me to explain this wastage of opportunity. Just ask the average young sportsman what he wants on tour. He'll say plenty of runs—or wickets—and a touch of the sweet life rather than a surfeit of sightseeing. I had better qualify that quickly. But after a tiring day in the field and with thoughts of a demanding schedule ahead, he is more likely to opt for a relaxing evening than a dutiful stop-off on the tourist route.

I had gone through my despondent moments both in India and Australia, when the runs refused to come. But the selectors appeared happy with my average and I was being told I could now establish myself in the Test side for years to come.

Ironic, isn't it, the way honours for my country have got obliterated in the Packer backlash.

But in 1976 life was beautiful and, as the embarrassingly kind civic reception committees at the airport back in Antigua seemed to suggest, Vivi was the boy to watch.

It was the turn of the Indians to come to the West Indies. I'm sorry to say it wasn't a good-tempered series. There were some pretty unpleasant jibes in the fourth and last Test at Kingston.

The Indians argued that our fast bowlers were intimidating them. No-one really enjoyed playing in that match. We won by ten wickets and certainly there were rather a lot of short-pitched balls. I didn't think they were particularly vicious. The varying bounce didn't help and some of the Indian batsmen got themselves into trouble.

Mike Holding was making them ping down and, I think he'd agree, was generally unloved by the Indian batsmen. Several of the tourists, including Gaekwad, who had made 81, and Patel, retired hurt and took no more part in the match.

There was a remarkable finish and I'll never see anything like it again. India's second innings closed at 97–5. None of us really knew what was happening. I'm sure the umpires and the crowd didn't. Later it was made clear that the rest of the side were 'absenting themselves'. Bedi put out an official statement saying the innings should be recorded as completed.

It was no way to round off the series. But the Indians, in my opinion, over-dramatised the dangers.

Andy Roberts missed the aggro at Kingston, at least as a player. He was feeling mentally and physically tired out and asked to be allowed to withdraw from the Test side after the first two Tests.

I could sympathise with him. Our schedule around the world was placing a terrific strain on the players.

Perhaps it was my mother's famous pepper-pots that I enjoyed so much on my weeks at home between cricket commitments. In any case I was escaping the jaded feeling that was knocking out some of our boys. I scored a century in three of the four Tests, at Bridgetown and twice at Port of Spain. I finished with an average of 92·66 and decided I was born lucky.

Not much sign of a let-up, though. We were due to tour England and that was going to be another crunch series.

Our manager Clyde Walcott made it clear that this wasn't going to be any rest-cure, tired as we might feel. We had lost badly to Australia and now we had to restore some prestige.

'If you lose to England, it'll go down badly at home', we were told. The message was clear and rather sinister. This was going to be a killer series.

5th Test, England v. West Indies at The Oval 1976. On the way to 291.

The English weather gave us a Caribbean welcome. It was the hottest summer for years there and we responded with the sun on our backs. The first two Tests were drawn and we won the last three.

Most of the players were still feeling sick about the way Australia had wiped the floor with us. We had a lot to prove. And we intended to let the ball fly faster than English batsmen had ever known before.

Mike Holding was on his first tour of England. He finished with 14–149 at the Oval. I think at times he frightened the daylights out of one or two of the English cricketers, brought up on the comparatively gentle pace of English county wickets.

Towards the end of May I'd come back to Taunton to play for the West Indies against Somerset. The locals were all hoping I would be in the side, which was nice. If they sensed that ours was an uncharacteristically subdued dressing-room it was only because we had acquired a pretty steely approach. Jokes were out.

I remember making 51 before 'Both' got one to move away and young Trevor Gard, the club's reserve wicket keeper given a game in place of Derek Taylor, took the catch. Ian and I exchanged a grin as I made my way back.

I'll never admire Closey more than in that match. He stayed for four hours 35 minutes to score 88. That was the skipper at his most cussed. He was determined to do well against us, whatever we threw down at him. He couldn't have imagined, however, what would happen. The gutsy knock won him a Test place again after nine years.

It was an incredible piece of selection, knowing the way selectors' minds work. My only criticism is that it didn't come a long time earlier. He was lost to the Test scene prematurely. He should have been captaining England. It wasn't fair on him that he was expected to pull it all out again when the pressures on him were enormous and he was facing some of the fastest bowlers in the world. As it was, he was as brave and stubborn as ever. My feelings were mixed when he walked to the wicket.

He and John Edrich had a rough time of it at Old Trafford where, it's true, the bouncers flew. Bill Alley, well known to me, of course, for his Taunton connections, warned Mike Holding after three short ones in a row. Andy Roberts deserved a hat-trick so much—and he would have had one if Gordon Greenidge, usually so reliable, had held a sharp chance in the slips.

I missed the Lord's Test because I was unwell. Apparently I caused a bit of a stir when a group of my friends from Bath knocked at my hotel bedroom door to enquire about my health. They were taken back to discover a lady in my room.

I can't wait to put the record straight. Friends used to come all the time to wish me well.

That day I can remember so well sitting on the side of my bed chatting to my sympathetic callers including one or two ladies.

I was far from well and feeling sorry for myself. Far too poorly, in fact, to divert from sickbed conversation. Sorry, lads, to ruin a good story back in the Lansdown club bar. . . .

For most of the time I was fit and frisky—at the wicket. I started with a double century in the first Test at Trent Bridge. And I rounded off the series with 291 at The Oval. My aggregate was 829 and my average 118·42.

Back in the Waldorf Hotel, where the West Indies side were staying during the Oval match, I had plenty of callers from my own Island. Someone claimed, 'Not only was your cousin there, Viv, but every Antiguan in Britain seemed to have found you out!' It was a crammed bedroom.

There was one dignified young man in a light-coloured suit who threaded his way through the crowd and congratulated me on my overnight score of 130 not out.

Afterwards I felt a bit of a rebuke in a friend's voice when he said, 'You just sat on the bed and stuck out a hand. Don't you know that was the Prime Minister's son?' No slight intended.

I hope I could be forgiven for the occasional lapse in coping with the social whirl around me.

My parents taught me how to behave in company. But they couldn't have been expected to tell me to get my weary legs off the bed when the Premier's son wanted to say 'Well done!'

My 291 at The Oval had to be one of the highlights of my still limited but eventful cricket career. As the innings went on and I

Acknowledging applause.

came in for the breaks, one or two grinned, 'You can crack Gary Sobers' record, Viv'.

I didn't want to hear that kind of talk. In the same way as when the papers made something of the fact that I'd whacked the best Test score by a West Indian in England since Sir Frank Worrell's 261 at Trent Bridge in 1950, I wanted to crawl into a corner. 'Never once during my knock', I assured the reporters, 'was I thinking about any kind of record.' If my cricket ever gets to that state I'll chuck it rightaway. That is not false modesty. At no time have statistics made any impression on me. Perhaps they should have, I don't know. I don't keep a scrap book or press cuttings.

Before I leave my Test career I must look back a season to cricket's first World Cup. The final of the Prudential Cup, as it was called, was memorable because it nearly had to be finished by candlelight. We started at 11 a.m. and Australia were beaten by a quarter to nine at night. Spectators said it was the most entertaining match they had ever seen.

Clive Lloyd, looking as studious as ever, rose to the occasion with a century. Less typically, Gordon Greenidge took 80 minutes over 13. And poor Roy Fredericks stepped back on to his wicket when hooking a bouncer for six. Gary Gilmour quickly bowled me and I was obviously being played for my fielding. At least. I ran three out.

Friends saw me on the television whooping with joy and they knew I couldn't hide my emotions all the time on the field. But, do you know, I got just as big a kick, the day we played Northern New South Wales out at Newcastle just before the Sydney Test, seeing my 'star', Andy Roberts, come on as substitute and get rid of four opponents in 20 minutes!

He wasn't in the side because he had a sore ankle. And I expect he hoped for a quiet time when he strolled on as substitute for a brief stint. Some hope—he started by catching Edwards and Wright, then ran out Howarth and Holland. We mobbed him and roared with laughter.

'We'll play you as sub again', we joked.

That Prudential Cup final was played on June 21, the longest day of the year. I could see why it needed to be. The competition was worth more than £200,000 in takings. It brought a new world-wide dimension to cricket. There were scenes of excitement more like a soccer crowd and I doubt if everyone approved. I sensed then that cricket was on the move. Leisurely three-day matches in England, played before a handful of spectators, were being overtaken.

As cricketers from the different countries talked together at the World Cup, they knew that the re-structuring of the game would continue.

Few realised the extent. Out in Australia, a burly, chain-smoking television tycoon was already hard at work on his brainchild.

My final West Indies commitment, after the England tour, was at home against the Pakistan tourists.

It was a series that I finished with my mind on other things.

With Packer

I've always tried to keep my distance from politics—and that also means those in cricket. It's hard not to become involved, voluntarily or otherwise, in party politics in an island like Antigua which is intensely political. When I'm asked for my opinion on a sensitive subject, I laugh or pretend I didn't hear the question. That doesn't mean I have no opinions of my own. It's just that I prefer to keep them private. Call me chicken if you wish; but a so-called sports celebrity can always be a useful political ally and I tactfully stay out. I couldn't be completely untouched by politics in a household like ours. My father numbers professional politicians among his friends. He has campaigned at election time. And it's far from good news domestically when his man loses.

As for cricketing politics, plenty of ideas have been flying round my head in the last two or three years. Most of them, of course, revolve around the name of Kerry Packer.

I have seen a good many newspaper reports which implied that it was a difficult decision for me to become a Packer man. It was confidently suggested at one time that I would readily opt out of the organisation at the time of my involvement with an Australian radio station.

My decision to join Mr Packer and his Cricket Revolution was one of the easiest of my life.

I was playing for the West Indies against Pakistan at the time in Trinidad. An agent from the Packer organisation approached several of us during the match. The others were, I believe, on that occasion Clive Lloyd, Andy Roberts and Mike Holding.

There had been all sorts of whispers that the game was poised for a business take-over like this. Professional cricketers had talked idly of a Super League—with its new rules and rich pickings. Most of us thought there were too many snags for the time being. We couldn't think who might have the initiative to organise a set-up which would turn the traditional game upside down and not be afraid to upset many people.

Most of the players felt they were grossly underpaid. I used to sympathise with county cricketers in England who had families to keep and weren't always sure of employment for the other six months of the year. It wasn't so bad for the young bachelors with no responsibilities. I must admit that when I entered county cricket in 1974, I didn't stop to worry about the meagre rewards. After all, I was getting such a kick merely from playing. And I was being paid at least something for playing the game I loved, the thing I could do best in life.

Cricketers are basically serious people. They are worriers. Get them together back in the hotel on a wet day—or sharing a pint with their opponents after the close of play—and they swop financial grievances. They belly-ache about the short duration of their playing careers and the need to make what they can from the game. Allowances and bonuses are important to them. I have seen some pondering over their car expenses with as much interest and care as if it were their batting averages. Such anxieties in a career, which at county level has not been renowned in the past for its generosity, is absolutely understandable.

In the sense that I now play in World Series Cricket and am paid for it on a par with a business executive, I suppose it's fair to call me a cricket mercenary. We are marketing our skills—and getting the best possible return for them.

I'm not by nature a grasping individual but on that hot afternoon in Trinidad when the Man from Packer got the three or four of us in a quiet corner and explained what he had to offer, my eyes lit up.

It's all very well to criticise us for not supposedly having the good of the game at heart and for not seeing any farther than the end of our cheque-book. Our ears have burnt as people have accused us of being avaricious, disloyal and completely insensitive to public opinion.

I never thought I'd hear so much hypocrisy in my life as what followed.

For the fact is this. Nine out of ten county cricketers in England would, at that time, have accepted the Packer terms on the spot if they had been offered them. They would certainly have been mad to refuse.

The terms, to me, as everyone seems to know by this time, were £25,000 for the first three years. No 'ifs' and 'buts' on the contracts.

Quite honestly I couldn't wait to sign. Nor could the others. I didn't need to consult my Antiguan legal adviser, Mr Christian, over this. The Packer agent spelt it out simply and clearly. Then he left us together to think about it. Clive Lloyd was a man I trusted implicitly. He looked at the rest of us and we knew from the way he nodded approvingly that he saw no loopholes. That was good enough for me.

I signed the Packer contract while I was still in the West Indies. Back in England, news of the Australian tycoon's coup was causing a furore.

Len Creed, who had continued to keep a hand on my shoulder, wanted to know what was going on. 'Don't panic, Mr Creed. I've signed for World Series Cricket, but I'll still be playing for Somerset.' That seemed to placate him although he and a good many others weren't at all sure what was going to happen and whether the Packer cricketers would be banished for ever.

The approach had been made at Port of Spain during the second Test. My last four innings in the series were 4, 33, 5, and 7. Not quite the consistency expected of a No. 3. Maybe my head was spinning at the new prospect opening up for me.

When news of the Packer plans later became public knowledge in England, friends started button-holing me at the county ground in Taunton. Some were very pointed in their advice. Many were well-meaning if, as I felt, misguided. As soon as I tried to assure them that it shouldn't affect my cricket for Somerset they seemed happy. Their concern was flattering.

Somerset, still with Brian Close as captain—it turned out to be his last season—were hoping to win something that summer. It was the season when Alec Bedser came down to watch them, picked Ian Botham for the next Test and pencilled in Brian Rose as well for the winter tour. A group of talented young West Country cricketers were emerging together. And I was seen as part of the Somerset success story.

Reporters were continually ringing me at my Taunton digs. No-one appeared to know how the law would stand. But never for a moment did I imagine that I should be banned from playing for my county. The Packer people, who had taken expert legal advice, subsequently borne out, had reassured us.

Although I'd taken a quick look at my contract for the World Series, I didn't intend to bother too much with the small print. Clive Lloyd seemed to think everything was in order. Frankly I couldn't see much wrong with the prospect of £75,000 going into my bank account.

Yet as the time to go to Australia drew close I did get some slight misgivings once or twice and wondered what I was letting myself in for. Some of the boys passed on hairy accounts of how the new wickets were supposedly being prepared. I was worried—the only thing I've ever demanded during my cricket life is a wicket that plays true. I've never once flinched from a ball, however fast it's been hurled at me, provided I've known that the pitch could be trusted. What should I expect in Mr Packer's Circus?

And what about the floodlights and the white balls? And an atmosphere which some people seemed to think would be more like show business than a cricket match? And how well would the players get on together, coming from different nations? Would we begin to act like a crowd of super-stars, losing the ability to enjoy a game we'd played in a certain way since schooldays?

The West Indian Packer players flew into Melbourne, rather quiet and not too certain what to expect. Our new employer was there to meet us. I was impressed with his size and his self-assurance. He immediately put us at our ease. He asked us if anything was worrying us; he showed great patience in answering our questions.

Kerry Packer had immense faith in his enterprise which reassured us. He knew he was taking on the entire cricket establishment. I got the feeling that he relished the challenge ahead.

I formed the impression that a great many people had got the wrong idea about him. He had been abused and insulted in the committee rooms and in print. He had been discourteously treated, as far as I could see, when he came to England to look for compromises. When he met us at Melbourne he was looking tired. He also looked like a fighter—and the West Indian boys admired that.

Off the field a kind of comradeship built up among the Packer players. Maybe we all felt rather like outcasts. At least that was what the big newspaper headlines suggested. We took a terrible battering in the press. That was particularly true of Mr Packer himself. Tony Greig, accused of helping to set up the whole operation in an under-handed way, was also being pilloried.

It was exciting for me to meet some of the great cricketers from different countries. Mr Packer organised a super dinner for all of us in Melbourne and when it came to Christmas Day, wives and girl friends were invited to join us for turkey and Christmas pudding. There was a new level of social life to go with cricket. We all knew that cricket could never be the same again. I don't think any of us had a single misgiving remaining.

The Packer wickets proved to be some of the best I have ever played on. The floodlights were no problem. After a time we weren't even conscious of the strange conditions. I'm convinced it's the best idea ever introduced to cricket. More experiments will probably be tried and conditions can only go on improving. The Australian climate, in particular, is absolutely right for the floodlit matches. I was able to pick up the white ball beaming through the air without any trouble.

And here's an interesting thing. We had time off and opportunities to live it up. I don't know if it was the thought of how much money we were now earning but we seemed to take on a new sense of responsibility. We knew what was expected of us, of course.

My first experience of Packer cricket left me with one

Above With my godchild, and Ian Botham.
Below Relaxing with Miriam in Taunton.

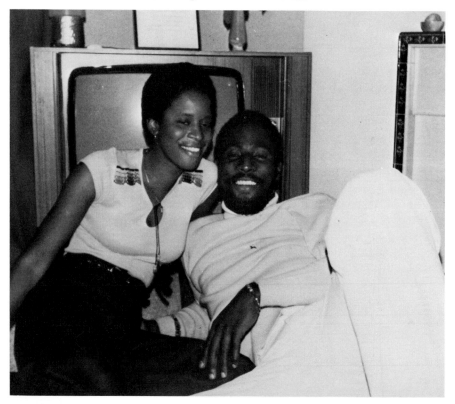

unwavering impression. This was the hardest and most competitive sport I'd ever played in my life. We were good players competing keenly for places. We all wanted desperately to be selected. We knew there was only one way we should be included—on merit. In no way could games against the Australians, for instance, be easy pickings. This brought an extra dimension to my play. The additional discipline I showed for Somerset in some of the 1978 Gillette Cup matches could be attributed largely to Packer.

It may sound corny to suggest that there was an atmosphere of a 'happy family' among the World Series players; but it was true. This did disappear, however, the moment we went on to the field. The 'needle' was important to the success of the series. Mr Packer didn't want the matches looking like friendly Saturday afternoon cricket with nothing at stake. On the field we bared our teeth.

Len Pascoe is a player who can hate you while the game is on. In one of the World Series Cricket matches he let go a couple of bouncers. I top-edged both of them for four.

He rushed down the wicket and said, 'Next time you miss, you'll be a hospital case.'

I said nothing. I glared back at him. Intimidation is part of the game and never affects me.

Pascoe has always been a highly competitive player. His threat was met by me in the most effective way I knew. I didn't miss the ball again.

I should, in fairness to him, say that he is as good as gold after a match. Like a number of the Aussies, he loathes the opposition—just as long as the game goes on.

But at least he also has a sense of humour. In that tense battle with me, after I had taken a succession of fours, he turned to Clive Lloyd, the batsman at the other end and said, 'This bloody bloke is playing by numbers!'

Ian Chappell is often considered abrasive and is far from loved by many of his opponents. His language is certainly ripe and there is an often-told story of a lively exchange he had in an Australian bar with Ian Botham in the days before the Somerset player was even considered a Test prospect.

Chappell, to me, is a gutsy chap. I have never had any trouble with him. I also have a great liking for his brother, Greg. We always had something to talk about—our days with Somerset. He looks back with affection to his brief stay in the West Country.

There's nothing necessarily wrong with an atmosphere of 'aggro' on the pitch. Anything that adds to the sharpness of the contest is good for the game. English county cricket has often seemed to me much too soft.

There's a tendency for pleasant 'Good mornings' and idle chatter immediately before play starts. Sorry, civilised England, but I don't want to know. The 'Good morning' nonsense irritates me. I simply want to get on with it.

In the same way there's a lot of chatting that goes on in county cricket during play. I don't join in. I mean the kind when the batsman takes guard and suddenly starts talking to the close fielder.

If I'm that fielder, at slip or gulley, I don't respond. And why? He's probably chatting away to me because he's nervous. Why should I put him at ease? My job is to help dismiss him. I'll be as friendly as the next man to that batsman—once we are back in the bar after the close of play.

Rodney Marsh is another Aussie who gives nothing away. He wasn't the most popular wicket keeper in my book on the second day of the Super Test in Melbourne. Nor was umpire Jack Collins who in the opening over had given out Gordon Greenidge LBW when it seemed apparent that he had hit the ball. Gordon didn't want to walk. That was a wicket to Dennis Lillee, who with Max Walker, soon had us in all sorts of trouble. Clive Lloyd came in 68–4 and the pair of us suddenly spurted ahead. I was on 79 and feeling in particularly good nick when I had to cope with a nasty turning ball from leg-spinner David Hookes. I edged it and Marsh missed the catch. But the ball lodged in his pads and, as he fell, frantically trying to keep the ball there, it rolled on to the ground.

Great juggling went on and it didn't look a clean catch to me. Rodney bellowed for a catch, arguing that it had wedged in his pads long enough. Jack Collins seemed in no doubt that I was out. As I spun round to see Rodney on the ground and the ball trickling away, I was a good deal less certain.

So there were a few disappointments for me. My overall performance for World Series Cricket was still the best in the party. At one time I had an average of just under 94.

I was told that Mr Packer considered I provided one of the best arguments for his new Circus. Certainly I had no difficulty making runs in the new conditions he had prepared for us. I responded to the challenge. Like most of the players I realised we had something to prove. We considered much of the criticism was unfair and often petty. Some of it seemed to spring from envy. And I didn't think that was a good enough reason for giving us a rough ride.

Freddie Trueman, who initially couldn't apparently make up his mind whether he was for or against us, soon turned up to commentate on our performances. He seemed to enjoy it and he nominated my 79 in the first Super Test as one of the greatest innings he had ever seen. I was more pleased with the 170 against the Australians in the final World Series match at Melbourne.

I gained a reputation as one of the big run-getters for Mr Packer. The hard, true wickets were right up my 'Antiguan' street. My timing has always been my strength and it didn't let me down. I suppose my lasting memory, despite the kind words of people like Richie Benaud and Barry Richards for other innings, was in the high-scoring match between the World XI and Australia at Perth. I'd made 72 by the end of the first day and went on to score 177 out of a mammoth total of 625. It was one of the games when I never felt I was going to be out; in fact Max Walker caught me eventually on the boundary when I thought I had got Lillee away for six. That particular knock took my aggregate to 1,064 runs and I was feeling rather pleased with myself. I don't often allow myself to be too generous about opposing bowlers but Ray Bright, I remember, deserved his 5–149 in that match for sheer perseverance.

But in the process of opting for Packer I had alienated myself from the West Indies Cricket Board of Control. This was really inevitable from the moment the six Packer players withdrew from the team to play Australia in the third Test, in Guyana, earlier in the year.

Board president Jeffrey Stollmeyer's statement was curt and to the point. 'In view of the decision of the World Series Cricket contracted players to withdraw from representing the West Indies in the Test match, the Board, in the interest of the future of West Indies cricket, has decided that these players will take no further part in the current series . . .'.

It was very sad. Players like Gordon Greenidge, Joel Garner, Colin Croft and Andy Roberts had achieved the proud ambition of being picked for their country. And suddenly, unnecessarily, everything had gone sour.

Our walk-out on the eve of the Georgetown Test was a dramatic and unhappy affair. It all started when Clive Lloyd resigned as skipper on a matter of principle. He was most upset that three Packer men, Deryck Murray, Richard Austin and Desmond Haynes had been dropped. The rest of us had a great deal of respect for, and loyalty towards, our captain. We had no doubt what was the right course for us. Unanimously we agreed to take 'industrial action'—we came out in sympathy with Clive.

Rumours were strong at one time that I was bidding goodbye for good to Mr Packer. In fact, most of the cricket writers in Fleet Street, as well as others in Australia and home in the West Indies, seemed to think I was giving a two-fingered snub to the man who was offering me a minor 'fortune' for playing the game his new way.

The confusion was caused because of my involvement with the Brisbane radio station 4IP, best known for the huge contract it gave Jeff Thomson. The station signed him up for ten years for a sum reported to be 633,000 dollars. For that, he was expected to play for Queensland and Australia. We've all heard of the unhappy developments since then in his case.

Alvin Kallicharran and Thommo were managed by an anti-Packer man, David Lord. So was I. When Alvin and Jeff pulled out of Packer, everyone assumed that I'd do the same. Mr Lord said, 'It took guts to do what Jeff did. He was one of Packer's biggest cards.' He confidently anticipated that I would bring added embarrassment to J.P. Sports Ltd. His reasoning was that I might lose money in the short term but not in the long.

One of the Brisbane radio station representatives, Frank Gardiner, was in England at the time. He spoke to me and did his best to influence me.

Meanwhile, down in Hampshire, Barry Richards, Gordon Greenidge and my mate Andy Roberts were making it clear they had no intention of withdrawing. Nor had the Gloucestershire pair, Mike Procter and Zaheer Abbas.

All of us were made to feel pretty uncomfortable. We were shocked by the venom shown against us by the International Cricket Conference. Anyone would have thought we were criminals. Mike Procter wasn't even in conflict with his country. They had already been boycotted because of their racial attitudes. I may not have had any sympathy for those; I had plenty for this fine all-rounder who at last had the chance of some international cricket in keeping with his talents. But he was being treated scornfully—not by Gloucestershire—simply because he had signed a contract, perfectly lawful, to be employed part of the year by a man who had dared to take on the establishment.

I found none of this vindictive reaction in Somerset. But I don't imagine Dennis Amiss felt the same, at times, about Warwickshire. I don't intend to go over all the old ground. I tried to wade through some of the words on the subject in the Daily Telegraph between innings. Sometimes I settled for the shorter version in the Sun, helped on my way with a quick glance at the non-cricketing page 3. Honestly, I couldn't believe it in the August when the Test and County Cricket Board decided to ban us all for two years, subject to the High Court ruling. We all know what happened in the High Court. I'm surprised more questions weren't asked about the money contributed by poverty-stricken county clubs to help pay the legal costs.

Even a simple soul like myself, unused to the ways of the law in Britain, felt that Packer was bound to win. I don't know what advice was given to those who fought the unsuccessful case. Maybe if they'd cooled it a little and not been so blindly cussed and heavy-handed, a lot of money wouldn't have been

Fellows of the 'Ovals' after a game of real cricket!
I am at the front next to Tohijo in the hat.

needlessly spent on expensive lawyers.

Many people wanted the World Series Cricket matches to
flop. They gloated when only 2,487 spectators saw the first day's
play of the Melbourne Super Test. True it went up to 5,088 on
the second day. Rockhampton attracted an attendance of 1,200.
And when an official Australia-India Test at Brisbane had
better crowds, the sceptics were having a ball.

Some of our crowds were a great disappointment to Mr
Packer, although the vastness of the stadiums made it look
worse. But we did pick up. There was a memorable one-day
match at Perth between the West Indies and Australia, watched
by well over 13,000. Joel Garner, later to join me with Somerset,
bowled particularly well to take four wickets. I hit an unbeaten

half century as we moved to a win by six wickets. And Dennis Lillee went to hospital that day with a badly sprained ankle.

It's all very well to say that 25,000 people saw the start of the Fifth official Test between Australia and India in Adelaide. Some of our one-day Packer matches, particularly those at night, were equally appealing. Who'll forget Barry Richards' 207 and Gordon Greenidge's 140? I didn't do so badly with a knock of 177 in a one-day match.

Under the moon and the floodlights in Melbourne we pulled in just under 25,000. This, many of us agreed, was where the future perhaps lay. Mr Packer was smiling broadly again.

Cricket at midnight? OK, I know it sounds absurd—but it works.

I shall be very surprised if Packer Cricket doesn't build on this success. It took imagination and guts (and money) to try it out. Now just watch how it takes off.

The way the players were recruited in the first place wasn't ideal. But soon there were 51 names—and very few faint hearts.

We were told, 'It's going to cause a rumpus for a time. Then the whole thing will blow over. There's no reason at all why county cricket in England, for example, should suffer at all.'

Some critics seemed to think we were indifferent to our various country and county commitments, that we were after a quick buck and were only too ready to turn our back on our old friends and responsibilities. Can you honestly believe that Kent players like Derek Underwood, Alan Knott and Bob Woolmer had such little regard for the side they had represented for years?

The Packer business has left bitterness in some cases. There have been divisions unnecessarily driven between a few players and their clubs. Countries have been deprived of some of their best cricketers.

When many of us returned to our English counties for the 1978 summer we weren't quite sure whether there would be a backlash of feeling. A few old die-hards were never going to forgive us, we discovered from the correspondence columns of the newspapers.

I can only report on my personal experience, back at Taunton, Bath and Weston. People, including other players, were interested and curious at first. They wanted to know about the white balls, the floodlights and the protective headgear. They wanted to know if I thought it would catch on.

Not a single person came up and criticised me for becoming a 'mercenary'.

And, as I rather expected, the topic of Packer was soon dropped altogether. By the time the county championship was under way and I was again buckling down at No. 3 for Somerset, everyone seemed to have forgotten all about the Circus—at least for the time being.

Whenever I had a chat with Joel Garner, Mike Procter or Bob Woolmer, we used to grin and wonder what all the fuss had been about. . . .

But, of course, it was back to Australia again towards the end of 1978. Would WSC confirm the bright and defiant start that it had made twelve months earlier? Would we even, as some seemed to be increasingly hoping, be prepared to kiss and make up with those die-hard cricket establishment figures who apparently thought we'd committed an unforgivable mortal sin? In fact, there wasn't much more than a hint or two of reconciliation. Hard-line attitudes appeared, if anything, to get harder. We had abrasive comments again from both sides and if olive branches were momentarily extended, they weren't exactly welcome. Why should Packer concede ground, anyway? His revolutionary approach to the game continued to gain spectacularly in popularity.

Floodlit cricket, WSC-style, was a dazzling success. Sydney's first fixture under lights attracted nearly 50,000 spectators. The match went out live to two and a half million on television. Others willingly paid up to £4 to attend. I had only one reservation about that particular match—Lillee got me for a duck.

Overall, the West Indians weren't always at their best in Australia. I had a few minor injuries and made a few bad shots. That was after I'd hit an undefeated 99 at Perth before I'd hardly got my kit out of my travel hold-all. But there were performances we could have done without. Like the day Greg Chappell and Gary Gilmour bowled us out for 66 at Sydney.

I managed one century in an unimportant match. I was more pleased with my 83 against a World XI, also in Sydney. That day I had a lovely vintage third-wicket stand with Clive Lloyd. And I remember collaring Derek Underwood to put a six away halfway up one of the huge Norfolk Island pines that encircle the ground. In the January we were again in dreadful trouble at 42–4 in Adelaide. Gilmour had got Desmond Haynes, Clive Lloyd and Jim Allen in a hat-trick. I decided to try to hit us out of trouble, made a quick 78 and we got home by two wickets.

Back in England the papers were still having a go at WSC whenever they had the chance. The critics wanted to know what this 'razzamatazz' had to do with the game they'd been brought up on. In Australia, we were being blamed for the decline of interest in the Sheffield Shield. A new public, including a lot of kids, were enjoying the ball game we'd introduced and this was also worrying the Australian Cricket Board who were pretty glum about the modest support for the official Tests.

The West Indies players with Packer allowed themselves a wry smile when they read that so-called antics weren't the exclusive right of WSC. There was Phil Edmunds pulling up his stump in a theatrical flourish because the bowling to him was so negative. And even the gentlemanly Mike Brearley was reportedly 'letting off steam' with my valued and occasionally volatile mate Ian Botham and John Lever. A bit sneaky of Gary Cosier, I thought, to relay that little dust-up on the field. These are happening all the time and no-one off the field is usually any the wiser. Cosier's 10-year contract, binding him to Queensland and Australia for the rest of his cricket career, came as something of a surprise to many of us.

I flew home to Antigua tired but in good heart. There was plenty of talk going on about what would—or might—happen over the World Cup. I left others to do the worrying. My only embarrassment was the fancy clothes we were now expected to wear in the interests of colour television. Cricketers in pink made me shudder a bit and I dared to tell Mr Packer so. You can imagine that we had to take some stick from those brash Aussie crowds!

I never doubted that the West Indies could take to WSC,

exciting and fiercely competitive as it is. The first Supertest was at Kingston, Jamaica, and we hammered the Australians by 369 runs. Clive Lloyd peered menacingly through his glasses to hit an unbelievable 197. And, wait for it, Andy Roberts (89) put on 226 with him for the sixth wicket. It was 33 more than he'd ever hit in a top match like this before. Hey, star, I'm going to have to watch it. Holding, Croft and Daniel tore through the Aussie batting.

On to Bridgetown, Barbados, for the second Supertest. The Aussies meant business by now. They made 311 and 296; we replied with 239 and 133–4. Full stop: match abandoned. Roy Fredericks, going like a bomb, was given out LBW. I was at the other end but, sorry, you won't prise any comment from me on that one. Too many dubious dismissals haunt me already. Well, Roy wasn't too pleased and nor was the crowd. There was bottle-throwing and chaos. Eventually the game was called off. A director of WSC, Austin Robertson had some pointed things to say and there was a statement put out by the two captains, Clive and Ian Chappell, implying that players who showed dissent wouldn't be considered for selection in the future. The third Supertest, at Port of Spain, was narrowly won by the Australians and again there was some crowd trouble. Play was held up for more than 20 minutes after Deryck Murray had been run-out.

But I was already convinced, spectator and umpire problems apart, that Packer had a place in the West Indies. And the fact that the final Supertest was due to be played in my own Antigua—on the St John's ground I knew and loved so much— already seemed like the fulfillment of a life's dream.

With My Own Thoughts

Do you know the most shattering experiences of my life? Not standing up to Thommo and Lillee or seeing the Gillette Cup and Sunday League slip agonisingly away from Somerset.

It was the days when Andy Roberts and myself stepped out of the aircraft into glaring sunlight at Coolidge—to be greeted, at different times, by two of Antigua's Prime Ministers, George Walter and Vere C. Bird.

We hadn't expected the red-carpet treatment. Suddenly it was there to welcome us, first when we came back from our initial tour in India, Sri Lanka and Pakistan, and then after we'd beaten England.

The pair of us had left for India, surprised that we'd even been selected. In my case, I thought I'd be found out—and wasn't going to be good enough. I dare say Andy felt the same.

Now we were back to what I suppose is called a hero's welcome. Everyone seemed to be at the airport. They were slapping us on the back as if we'd won the series on our own. We were taken to the VIP lounge and feted. They told us Antigua was proud of us. Photographers' bulbs were flashing all round and reporters from our local papers were plying us with questions.

We blinked a bit in the fierce sunlight and I don't expect we were too articulate. They asked about the Indian spinners and the crowd riots. About Andy's wickets and my runs.

The two local lads had returned home after representing their country at cricket. We sensed the honour that was being handed out to us . . . from the Prime Minister, the Minister of Sport and members of the Antigua Cricket Association downwards. We felt grateful, confused, overawed—and we couldn't wait to creep away from the well-intentioned welcoming committee and the smiling onlookers, to see our families again.

I remember looking at Andy in almost a state of panic, as if to say, 'Hey star, what have we done?'

It was frightening me. My startled eyes darted round the scores of familiar faces at the airport. Many of them were genuine friends and great cricket fans. A few, I've no doubt, were among those who came round to my house and cat-called me after I'd got myself suspended.

I'm not knocking the warmth and the kindness of the people who were there to meet me. I was close to tears. And I knew that no island but Antigua could have shown such sincere delight and appreciation for a couple of young, unworldly cricketers who had made the Test team.

But I wasn't sure whether I could live with it. I lay on my bed that first night back in Drake Street and tried to analyse what was happening to me. It was one thing to be mobbed by your mates back in the bar after swinging a few carefree sixes at the Recreation Ground here in St John's. It was quite another when you suddenly found yourself wedged in by what seemed like nearly every resident in Antigua, as soon as you stepped out of the plane.

I don't know what I expected. Certainly not crowds or photographers' bulbs. Perhaps just a kiss from Miriam. Certainly not the official state car and a motorcade from the airport to my home. Not speeches and steelband music. I looked at that gleaming official car and thought to myself, 'I'll be lost in something as big as that.' So I asked for Miriam to accompany me on the heady ride home.

The Antiguan government is apt to give public holidays for the big cricket matches. It seemed to me, by the size of the crowd, that everyone was on holiday when we arrived.

You must remember that I was never fired with grand ambitions of playing for the West Indies. I had my normal fantasies as I played in the backyard with brother Merv and stalked to the improvised wicket as if I was Everton Weekes in one of his killer moods. But it didn't enter my head that I would get beyond the Island team. How often did Antiguans play for the West Indies anyway?

For Antigua to have two of us making the Test team was, I accept, something to celebrate.

But I wasn't ready for what was to follow. 'Listen, Vivi, you're a celebrity.'

In the next two or three years it was a strange, sometimes unnerving, process. Everyone started recognising me. Many wrote to me, 'Dear Viv, we enjoyed your knock . . .'.

The heads of Andy and myself appeared on the local postage stamps. We had free admission to the cinemas and were invited to many of the big hotels, places we'd thought were way out of our financial and social range before. We seldom had to buy a drink; we were invited to some of the restaurants and the bill was waived.

There were television appearances and at parties Andy and I were apparently considered prized guests.

But I tended to keep away from the big hotels with their passing tourist trade. Accents that belong to America or Germany rather than Antigua don't mean so much to me. They lack the local colour and the banter that only the islanders understand.

It's different in Albur's, the St John's disco. And different in the Golden Peanut Restaurant in the High Street. This is where I go most lunch-times when I'm at home. I'm still treated as one of the boys from the grammar school who hasn't really been away.

With Andy, when he's around, I turn up for my lobster sandwich or hamburger. Rolston, the proprietor, has a table specially reserved for us. I fancy one or two of the regulars get a bit annoyed that their seats have been taken away from them.

There we stay for up to two hours. The table gets crowded with happy cricket fanatics, many of them older men. They pull our legs. They don't care a damn that we've played for the West Indies. We're still two hopefuls from the Island, being given some stick by old friends and neighbours who make sure we don't get any big ideas just because we've had a few games around the world.

After a time our companions hurry back to work. They've come for the chat as much as a drink. And they go away chuckling.

'Young Vivi hasn't changed much,' is what I like to hear them say as they leave.

We drain our glasses, probably a fruit punch at that time of the day, and Rolston shouts across:

'Same time tomorrow, stars. Same table.'

A chat at Albur's or the Golden Peanut—and plenty of solid home cooking in Drake Street—is part of the fun of going home to Antigua. I still wake early and sometimes drive the few miles out to Fort James for some jogging. The legs—and inclinations—are more reluctant than they once were.

Public recognition, whether by a cop in Kent or a foreigner at the exclusive Mill Reef club in Antigua is something I don't easily take to. Some guys, sportsmen or pop stars, can swing along with it. They are outward-going and can't have too many headlines.

I'm made differently. When I turned up in England first and had my digs in Bath I was virtually anonymous. No-one had ever heard of me. That suited my personality, whatever the occasional strains on my home-sickness. In Taunton I value above all the privacy of my little flat.

During the 1978 season I received an incredible invitation. In a way it typified the dangers of becoming a so-called celebrity.

The letter arrived at the county ground in Taunton and it was written by a bloke from Grenada now living in England.

He said some nice things about my cricket. And then he asked, 'Would you attend my wedding? It would be the best possible present for my wife to have you at the reception.'

Vivian Richards as a wedding present? Now I've heard it all.

I wrote back politely pointing out that I should already have left England by the date of the marriage.

Now I know what some of you are going to say. What's wrong with a bit of fame when it boosts the bank balance?

It's a fair point. From 1976, in particular, I've become a very marketable person. I'm used to launch new beers and new bats. Unlike county cricketers in England who, in some cases, have the humiliation of going on the dole, I play all the year round—and get paid for it. I pick up generous cash prizes and dozens of perks. Packer has turned me into a big money-maker.

. . . So, I agree, why ever do I dare to say I can't stand the glare of publicity?

Of course, I'm not going to be such a hypocrite as to imply that I don't like the benefits that I suppose have turned me into one of the bigger cricket wage-earners in the world. I'm just trying to be as honest as I can and tell you how I struggle temperamentally to come to terms with it.

World Series Cricket has to be my main source of income. That offer of £25,000 a year put my head in a spin. Friends who knew I could be a bit of a spendthrift advised, 'Get someone to look after your money for you, Viv.'

My lawyer in Antigua has assisted me. So, as a convenience while I'm playing in England, has the manager of a bank several miles out of Taunton. Brian Langford, the former Somerset captain and off-spinner, put me on to him. 'Your affairs are a private matter. Take them outside the town where you work,' he said.

From time to time during my summers in England I put my black executive's case in my car and drive off. The lads at the county ground give me a grin. 'See you at the board meeting,' they say.

So I leave others to advise about investment and such things. In St John's for a time, Andy Roberts and I financed a sportswear and equipment shop. Miriam did the books and we hoped it would take off more than it did. It was never too easy when we were away so much of the time.

At the moment I'm thinking of switching to what the English call the rag-trade. My own interest in clothing could be the basis of a future business enterprise. I see a lot of things in Britain, involving the fashion business, that I'd like to introduce at home. Remember, people in Antigua like to dress well. It's a characteristic of the island. Not just a streak of vanity on my part.

Quite apart from Packer, my kind of cricket has brought me a succession of cash bonuses. The 1977 Bonusbond £1,500

Cricketer of the Year Award must have pleased my accountant. There was £500 from the People newspaper for my 73 sixes that same summer. It was, they told me, a world record previously held by another Somerset man, Arthur Wellard. At the county ground in Taunton, old supporters said Arthur used to like to hit the ball over the hoardings into the river and that a boat had to be kept handy when he was batting. He's my kind of cricketer.

There were other newspaper prizes including £500 for the Sunspots' Big Hitters. And £250 for hitting more boundaries than anyone else in the Tests when we played England. The next three in that competition? Gordon Greenidge, Roy Fredericks and Clive Lloyd. Tony Greig, I noticed, was the most successful of the England batsmen.

I picked up my quota of Man of the Match and gold awards and, as usual, half went into the players' pool. After one or two Gillette matches I was almost smothered with shaving equipment.

A stamp firm, Urch-Harris, decided to sponsor me for every run I scored for Somerset in 1978, 79 and 80. The chairman of the company, who has been a member of Somerset for nearly 40 years, said he was ready to cheer every innings. There can't be much wrong with the British economy when it's as fair-minded as that!

All this—and more—adds up, I accept, to a pretty good return for tonking a cricket ball around the ground.

I'm expected to pose for a few publicity pictures, for Skol beer or for the products of the latest donor. Most of this is written into my contract. When I go out to the wicket my Stuart Surridge bat is there for all, including the TV lens, to spot.

The Stuart Surridge Jumbo served me very well for most of 1978, until my fit of pique in the dressing room!

I'm not a superstitious cricketer. Unlike some West Indians and many British sportsmen I have no worries about the order in which I go on to the field or which boot to lace up first. It so happens that some seasons I stick to the one bat. But there's no firm rule about that. I'm happy to pick up the nearest to me— provided it bears the right label! If it's a short-handle, it'll do the job for me.

Cricket success has brought me free cars. My green Capri at Taunton came from Ford's. And when it took the plunge over the embankment on the M4 motorway, Somerset motor dealer Peter White, a squash-playing friend of mine, donated another Capri, caramel-coloured this time.

I suppose I'd better tell a story against myself, about the day I picked up my first car. It was a proud moment. The model, gleaming bright as I posed for the local photographers, had a nice sporting style to it.

I had brought Hallam along with me for my maiden ride. He jumped in alongside me in the passenger seat. Rather apprehensively I turned the ignition key and let out the clutch. Smoothly we purred away as the garage staff looked on approvingly.

'This is the life,' Hallam said, turning the window down. There's nothing quite like a smart new car for making you feel good. But then I made my big motoring mistake. I pulled into a self-service garage and, with the air of someone who had done it for years, filled up with fuel. The trouble was that I blissfully settled for two-star petrol. Soon the car was pinking badly and, after taking advice, I had the embarrassment of watching all the petrol being changed in my tank.

I've driven thousands of miles since then in a dozen different countries—and I've never again been too mean at the pumps. . . .

My dashing two-seater is now very much part of my lifestyle.

Life is sweet in many ways. I try to keep an eye on my chequebook although I've a tendency to go haywire on my spending. I buy clothes with reckless abandon and am shocked when I get the bill. But I ponder my responsibilities, including those to my family at home.

My parents are comfortably off. They were generous to me with pocket money in the days when I lazily put off any decision about going to New York to get my head down at night school. They also taught me to pay all my debts. I don't like to owe anyone. In the same way that I don't like too many friends to get a round of drinks without taking a turn myself at the counter.

You can ask them in the Stragglers' bar at the Taunton ground, or the Gardeners Arms.

I'm often encircled by friends. Just think of the Waldorf Hotel bedroom during the Oval Test when it was light-heartedly claimed that every Antiguan in Britain had squeezed in. I have a stack of genuine friends at Bath and Taunton, the kind for whose kids I willingly take an autograph book around the world (and then get it stolen from me in Australia). There are the hangers-on, too. Everyone in sport gets them. They talk as though they've known you for years. It isn't easy losing them.

Perhaps I should now come to the girls. Every West Indian cricketer is supposed to have magic powers when it comes to the chicks. The stories get back to us. Mostly they are to do with our so-called prowess. I will only say that a few tales of sexual athletics in Australia have a vaguely authentic ring.

West Indians are by nature a sexy race. Above all, they don't want to be talked about as failures in their relationships.

There's nothing more humiliating than for a West Indian to have his girl taken away from him, because he doesn't make it sexually, by another bloke. From that moment he's looked on as a joke. Life can be cruel. Virility is one of the main yardsticks among West Indian men.

Groupies exist in cricket just as in the pop scene. This is particularly true in Australia and at home. We turn up at the same grounds and know that we'll see the same pretty faces hanging around afterwards. And some not so pretty.

A few of those pale Aussie faces haunt you. You go back the next time and they are looking just as pale and lost. Permanent relationships usually elude them.

In their desperation they sometimes go to extremes. Both in Australia and England girls have come up to me and asked for my autograph. But wait, they have asked me to sign their breasts. It isn't my scene. That to me is ugly and I turn away. I may not be quite the most lily-white cricketer on the circuit but I've got a strong Puritan streak and maybe should thank my Victorian parents and the cathedral choir for that.

I enjoy the company of young ladies. Once, as I changed after a match at Taunton on a Saturday night, I remember a friend saying to me, 'There are five of them out there waiting, Vivian.' That didn't mean I was a sex maniac. They happened to be five friends waiting to have a drink and a chat with me.

In Britain I have a dozen or so girls who mean a good deal more to me than a one-night stand. I keep phone numbers religiously and when we're playing away I ring for a date. There are good friends in Nottingham, Cardiff, Birmingham, Manchester, London and, of course, Taunton.

After a game of cricket I prefer the company of girls. It's the perfect relaxation for me. I like to do the running. Cricket as a subject is taboo.

My interest in them wanes if they have no conversation nor a sense of humour. These are essentials. Some of them take me home to meet their parents. Occasionally I take them to my flat to play records. One or two get things, emotionally, a little bit out of control. They have even talked about marriage. The odd girl has tried gentle blackmail but I make no promises.

I've remained good friends with most of the girls I've met at some time in Britain. They know my attitude to life. If I ever thought one was going out with me because I've got a reputation of being a useful cricketer, I'd stand her up.

I make no excuse for enjoying the good life. I detail it here only because it's part of me, part of the West Indian style. Morally I have never done anything I am ashamed of. Nor has a pretty girl ever got in the way of my next innings.

Any girl friends I have had when playing away from the West Indies have known that the affection could only be temporary. My relationship back in St John's with Miriam is different and deeper. I hope that doesn't sound like something out of a woman's magazine. It happens to be true.

I've still got some way to go to reach 30. My personality will go on maturing and changing. Maybe I'll cut down on the late nights although my head buzzes unto the early hours and I can never drop off. How hard I tried before that Essex semi-final match. Curry take-away and back in bed by ten. And I hardly slept all night.

I'm a mixture, certainly. As a person I'm still shy, staying in the corner on the social occasion and refusing to have my name

153

splashed around on any publicity stunt. I hate being mobbed when I've done well. Maybe it gets misunderstood just occasionally. One Sunday late in 1978 Pete McCombe told his two small daughters to say, 'Good luck, Viv' just as I was about to leave for the match. Nothing could have been nicer or more touching than that.

But they caught me on the hop. About a dozen or more of their young friends, all under ten, were there with them. They wished me good luck in unison.

I can't say why but I was embarrassed. I turned to Pete and said, 'That's the last time I'm coming round to your house.'

People who make a fuss about any successes I may be having make me angry. I get the impression that sometimes they are more anxious to bask in the show themselves. Bad umpires also make me see red—but only for five minutes. One of my own irresponsible shots, when there is no need, upsets me. I don't regret smashing the door at Harrogate or my bat at Taunton. They were releasing my emotions.

I'm easy to get on with in the dressing room. If there's any back-biting, I keep away from it. I don't often tell a joke myself but I'm always ready to share one with the other players. There is no county I should want to play for other than Somerset.

I expect a few of my whims intrigue the other players. From the days in Bath when I trudged round to the launderette and the dry-cleaners, I have tried to be as immaculate in my appearance as possible. Personal cleanliness is almost a fetish. They tell me I'm one of the few county cricketers who cleans his teeth after ever meal during a match.

My slight beard has been grown since coming to England. Maybe I was trying to make myself a little more manly! I trim it myself conscientiously. And I usually bring out the scissors to cut my own hair, although I have a very good hairdresser in London. Yes, he's an Antiguan.

In the few years since I've been paid to play cricket I've got wiser but my attitudes haven't changed. My politics are the same, even if no-one will ever prise them from me. I was once asked to talk to a League of Youth in Antigua. I made sure I chatted about cricket—and not the ruling party of the time.

If there's a hint of extra weight around my middle, put it down to my mother's baking and not that extra gin-and-tonic. Training comes harder, all the same. I've lost that old appetite I used to have for pounding along the beaches at home.

Like a few of my West Indian friends I believe in living hard and playing hard. It's a dangerous philosophy but, I argue, only in the long term.

I'm a happy person and I hope this is reflected in the way I play my cricket. Just once or twice the sport has got on top of me. I do worry about the effects of playing round-the-year. There's even a fear that I might become bored.

During one spell in Australia, when I was struggling for runs and confidence and my morale was sagging, I went to see a doctor and he put me on to Arthur Jackson who specialises in lifting the spirits of athletes when they are down. We decided my problem was psychological.

Perhaps because of my experiences then, I was able to be of some help to David Gurr, the young Somerset fast bowler, when he seemed to lose every bit of confidence after bowling a frightening succession of wides early in the 1978 season.

David is an intelligent young man who had started as a theology student at Oxford. We all thought he had a lovely action and when he lost his way, threatening to get into the Guinness Book of Records for the number of wides he sent down in a 2nd XI match, we tried to help him.

Peter Robinson, the coach, and chairman Roy Kerslake attempted to encourage him. They reminded him that a fine Somerset allrounder and former captain, Maurice Tremlett, once had the same trouble. The club doctor talked to him and I got him on one side.

I explained how several of the West Indies and Australian players, as well as Bob Willis, were helped by this chap in Australia. It was all a matter of acquiring extra concentration. David was then only 22 and, having left Oxford early, he was desperately keen to succeed as a county cricketer.

He ended up by visiting a psychiatrist. And by the end of the season he was back in the Somerset side, looking the best bowler on the field in the match with Gloucestershire at Bristol.

Like few other sports, cricket drains a player mentally. That's why I must make sure I don't get jaded.

But how long shall I go on playing? I can't be sure how much I shall be enjoying the game or how well I'll be whacking the ball in a few years' time. At the moment I enjoy it very much indeed—and that means with Somerset as much as with World Series Cricket.

I can't see myself going on beyond 35. Certainly I don't want to continue until I'm playing from memory. I've never looked on cricket as anything but a short life—and a fabulous one.

And this is the moment when I do my day-dreaming. I hope, when my county and Packer career is over, to return to Antigua. My idealistic plan is to do everything I can to encourage youth cricket on the Island. I should like to gather together fifteen or so of the most promising young players and form them into a permanent squad. Their only qualifications would have to be that they are Antiguans and that they love the game.

I'd then tour around with them. In that way the future of first-class cricket in Antigua would be assured.

Every time I go back to St John's and look in at the Recreation Ground I get excited. Big improvements are going on. The dressing-rooms alone are better than at any county ground in England.

Andy Roberts and I feel honoured that our names are commemorated in the pavilion renovations.

I hope to be part of that great new campaign for Antiguan cricket. The WSC Supertest was only a start.

That will be the day. Talk about public holidays.

Some of the money I have earned from the game will hopefully be ploughed back into the sporting future of Antigua. Up to now I have done some sponsoring of young cricketers and footballers. I'm also funding a basketball team in St John's called Vivi's O'Jays. When I'm home I go up into the park and we practise together. All the youngsters are friends and they come from my district.

Basketball? Yes, another of my old pastimes. I played for one of the top teams on the Island. The Knickerbockers. I wasn't quite the tallest player around but they said I made a good height. I should also say that I was then much slimmer.

Test cricket on the Recreation Ground . . . and fun in the park with Vivi's O'Jays or happy memories swapped with the 'Ovals' gang of boys. Do you get the feeling I'm already drifting back home in spirit? I can't deny it. After all I haven't had a Christmas with the family for six years. Come to that, I haven't managed to vote, either.

There is also the matter of starting a family. Even so-called international cricketers are capable of being sentimental.

The last thing I want to suggest is that I'm ready to chuck cricket—and head for home. I'm determined to win something for Somerset first and say thank-you to the county that gave me the encouragement I needed, as well as the necessary shop window.

If I'd stayed in Antigua, I don't think the selectors would have even noticed me. And who knows where I'd have ended up if I'd taken Big 'D's' sound advice and become an electrical engineer in massive, soulless, non-cricketing New York?

I'm realistic enough, though, to accept that by the time I'm 35—not old for a cricketer—I'll possibly have had enough. From then on, it'll be back to a few gentle swipes at the weekend for Rising Sun or one of the clubs I knew so well before.

It sounds mad but I'm not a travelling man. I get in and out of jets and never have time to go to the countries I want to visit.

I hate it in the air. Planes terrify me. When I go on tour Roy Fredericks usually sits next to me and he suffers agonies. I jump up and throw my hands about. The other boys know how nervous I get.

It goes back, I think, to when the Grammar School went to play soccer in Trinidad. I thought my number was up that day. The plane developed some mechanical trouble and, as far as I could see, only just managed to touch down. I kept looking out of the window of the plane, seeing it losing height all the time. It was a nasty feeling. And I think I had a rotten game.

I'm always in an aircraft nowadays and every flight is going to be like that journey to Trinidad. I look at the old labels on my baggage and marvel where I've been.

'And what's the Black Hole of Calcutta like then, Vivi?' they ask me over the hamburgers at the Golden Peanut.

I can't tell them. I'm never there long enough to find out—even if I wanted to.

Instead I tell them what Clive Lloyd's double century was like . . . and the way Lance Gibbs went into the record books.

One day I'll be able to throw away my suitcases and travel bags for good. Then, hopefully, I'll start catching up on all the letters that at the moment remain unanswered. I have some guilt about this. The mail is arriving for me all the time—from all over the world. There are the invitations to speak at dinners (as well as attending strangers' weddings as the special present!) I don't have the luxury of a secretary and few of the intended replies go off. Forgive me, reader, if yours is still waiting.

Nature made me a good cricketer—but a lousy correspondent.

As a cricketer, it came easily to me. God gave me a sharp eye and a natural sense of timing.

Roy Marshall, who arrived from St Thomas, Barbados, and went on to play brilliantly for Hampshire, runs a pub in Taunton these days. He went on television in England and said I hit the ball harder and with greater ease than anyone else he had ever seen.

That was flattering to hear. I hit the ball harder because I am strong and confident. I don't fear the bowler and don't think about him until I reach the crease. If he starts by giving me a bad ball I try to put it away for four.

I'm proud of my cover drive and the one that hums back over the bowler's head. No-one ever showed me how to play my best shots. Malcolm Richards and Alf Gover and Pat Evanson and Tom Cartwright and Brian Close and Peter Robinson, in their different ways, helped my by getting my feet right or telling me there was no virtue in trying to lose six balls every over.

Fielding was never a bind—except when I had a hangover at Weston-super-Mare! I used to field in the covers. The West Indies put me at slip and gulley. If I tended to doze when I came to Somerset first, Brian Close shook me out of that.

As to my off-spinning, opinions are apt to vary in Somerset

and I stick mostly to gentle seamers. Dare I quote from a report of the Leeward Islands' match with M.C.C. in Antigua after I'd completed my qualifying year with Lansdown:

> Roberts was rested and his replacement Richards made a vital break-through when he bowled Amiss for 44. Richards turned an offbreak up the slope and knocked over the off-stump . . .

When I played for Somerset in 1974 journalists began writing about my sunny approach and youthful grins on the field. They were only half right. I seldom grin during a match.

Whether I'm playing pool, basketball or cricket I want to give nothing away. I save my natural sense of friendship for off the field. That's an attitude I share with the Aussies.

Cricket has made me well-off and, I suppose you could say, worldly.

It has enabled me to play alongside the greatest cricketers in the world. I have done it in my own way, instinctively, still flashing at the ball at times when I shouldn't. I shall go on making mistakes and wanting to smash my bat afterwards. I hope I shall go on giving pleasure—for those who watch me in the West Indies, England and Packer country.

What I have tried to do in this book is explain myself as a person as much as a cricketer. I've traced my unexceptional background in Antigua, my chance coming to England and the way in the following years of international cricket I've been left almost bemused, swept along by a mixture of luck, suspense and dedication.

I've attempted to be honest with myself, acknowledging that I've enjoyed the good things in life. They have left me with plenty of warm friends and an occasional thick head for the early overs of the day. I have accepted discipline and never given less than my best on the field.

The generous words of Clive Lloyd, Brian Close and Colin Cowdrey have all helped at their different times. The no-nonsense advice and guidance of my parents has kept my feet on the ground. The ribbing of old friends around the table at the

Golden Peanut have been good for my soul.

Success, if that means hundreds in Wisden and a place on Mr Packer's pay-roll, has come quickly and dramatically to me. 'You're a star, Vivi,' they tell me when I go home.

Accomplishment to me hasn't got much to do with statistics. It's being around, all Packer antagonism forgotten I hope, when Antigua has its first Test match.

That will be fulfilment. Cricket will be beautiful. The Recreation Ground will be beautiful.

And if any bloke with a long memory mentions my suspension on this same ground, I'll hit him for six over extra cover . . . .